SON OF TOMMYWOOD

From Award-Winning Journalist and Producer

The Second Installment of the ***TOMMYWOOD*** Series,
a Collection of Columns and Writing on Arts and Culture

A PONDWOOD PRESS BOOK

PONDWOOD PRESS
1424 4th Street, Suite 229
Santa Monica, CA 90401

FIRST TRADE PAPERBACK EDITION

The majority of the articles in this collection first appeared in print in *The Jewish Journal of Los Angeles*, some in slightly different form and can also be found at tommywood.com.

ISBN: 978-0-9883964-6-3

Set in Minion
Printed in the United States

For Amy and Natasha

CONTENTS

INTRODUCTION

In this, the second collection of columns covering the period from 2005 to 2007, TOMMYWOOD really hits its stride. Two of the profiles, one on Susanah Hoffs and the other on Larry David, each won first place awards at the Southern California Journalism Awards hosted by the LA Press Club. The David piece, "Larry David Died for Our Sins," also won the Simon Rockower Award of the American Jewish Press Association.

It's a funny thing, before Tommywood, I had never written a column on a regular basis (although during law school I wrote one on an occasional basis). However, once I began, the column created its own discipline and rhythm.

As I look over these columns what strikes me is how personal they are. This collection begins with my sharing what it was like to grow up Jewish in New York and concludes with Los Angeles described as a city where one should "assume everyone is Jewish." It is a vision that is meant as expansive, not reductive; confident and proud. Not unlike the column.

In this volume there are a great many columns that mattered to me, whether it was about a post-Katrina New Orleans, the importance of Jerzy Kosinski's *The Painted Bird,* or to pay obituary tribute to Simon Wiesenthal. Tommywood became the place to make the case for Jewish Journalism or share my thinking about the Holocaust. I could in one column look back to a movie that made me laugh as a child, *The Mad Adventures of Rabbi Jacob* or write about Etgar Keret, an Israeli writer who was just becoming known in the U.S.

I championed writers whose work deserved to be better known such as Vassily Grossman, the great Soviet journalist and novelist and celebrated the work of my friends such as David Margolick, Seth Greenland, Jonathan Rosen, Jonathan Shapiro, Steve Rubin, Bruce Goldsmith, Nessa Rapoport. Tommywood also allowed me to write about people I always wanted to meet such as Phil Rosenthal (of *Everybody Loves Raymond*), Albert Brooks, and David Mamet.

Tommywood continues to be of Los Angeles: What we bring to it and what we take away from it, with a dollop of Hungarians thrown in for good measure.

If, in the words of Wordsworth, "the Child is father of the Man," then surely, I am the proud parent of *Son of Tommywood.*

Enjoy!

THE WAY IT WAS

Last week, playwright Donald Margulies, The Manhattan Theater Club and The Forward weekly newspaper announced the winners of a contest they sponsored on the topic of "What It's Like Growing Up Jewish in New York."

You can read the winning entries at www.forward.com. I regret to say you will not find my name among them (what do they know?). Still, my great consolation is being able to share my account with you:

Growing up Jewish in New York as the children of refugee émigrés, as the first generation born since the Holocaust, was, for me and my playmates on West End Avenue, like living a Mittel European version of the American dream. Anything good was possible; anything bad could never happen again.

There were no barriers to achievement. Every child could grow up to be the president of the United States, but we were told we would be doctors and lawyers. We would have an education, the best education. We would go to the best schools, the best colleges, the best graduate schools. We would get the best grades. We would study harder than everyone else, but we wouldn't have to, because it would come easy. American schools, we were told, weren't that hard.

Learning foreign languages would be no problem—our parents spoke six, seven, eight of them. We already understood more than they thought we did. They would speak to each other in Polish, in Hungarian, in German, in Hebrew and Yiddish, but not for much longer. Soon everyone would speak English.

There was nothing to be afraid of. They laughed. But they worried. All the parents worried. We knew that bad things had happened over there. We lost people. They were never seen again.

It wasn't exactly clear what had happened, but it had to do with the Nazis. That we knew. The Germans did it. But everyone we knew spoke German. So how could I know that someone wasn't really a German spy?

We called our grandmothers Oma. Those of us that had grandmothers. I didn't know anyone who had a grandfather. Everyone had people they called "Uncle" and "Aunt." Very few people had actual uncles and aunts. I couldn't figure out what a cousin was.

My friend's mother had numbers tattooed on her arm. Her mother told her it was her telephone number in Europe, and her mother had written it on her arm in case she got lost. Now it didn't rub off—another reason we shouldn't write on our arms.

Sometimes, parents screamed at each other. Some parents screamed at their kids. We walked on tiptoes. Our parents were strange sometimes. My father had nightmares. He screamed out in his sleep. I never asked the other kids if their parents screamed, too. But I could tell they did.

Our parents seemed brighter, smarter, sharper than other kids' parents or the parents on TV—they were older, too. Our parents' apartments were dark: filled with heavy furniture, thick rugs, ornate glass chandeliers and knickknacks everywhere.

They knew about rugs, jewelry, porcelain, paintings. They took us to art galleries, museums and pastry shops. They loved cookies and pastries. They drank tea, because the coffee was no good in America.

They knew about winter sports, such as ice skating and skiing, but nothing about sports such as football and baseball.

In some ways, the best part of growing up Jewish in New York was that our parents could live like they were in Europe without having to be there. Vienna, Budapest and Warsaw were all recreated on the Upper West Side.

Broadway had several Hungarian restaurants, such as the Emke and The Tic-Tac. There was the Hungarian Businessman's club to go play cards. One need not go for too long without Vienner schnitzel or cherry strudel.

Unlike other generations of immigrants, they did not have to leave who they were behind. Although my father arrived in New York with little money, he was still accorded respect for who he was and what he had done. "Herr President," a man greeted him on West End Avenue. At the Éclair Pastry shop, they wouldn't take his money. He insisted. They refused and so it went.

Certain things were too American. Or only for Americans. Americans spent money on stupid things. Americans liked senseless gadgets. American were fooled by labels—they didn't understand quality.

Growing up Jewish in New York, as the first generation born since the Holocaust, meant that we watched and listened and learned. We were the translators of the New World for the Old. We had to play by their rules, live their dreams, while carving out our own.

Our parents saw ladders everywhere—if you lived on the Upper West Side, you hoped to one day move to Central Park West or, if you could, to the East Side. That was the dream. Everything was a sacrifice "for the kinder"—for us. We were the hope, the pride, the point—the revenge and answer to what had occurred. Everything was for us and we would achieve it all.

We were Americans, after all, native born New Yorkers.

March 10, 2005

WOODMAN RETURNS

At the end of Woody Allen's *Melinda and Melinda,* I sat in my seat stunned: Woody Allen had actually made a movie I liked—a good movie that had something to say about life and literature. It felt like a long time since I'd enjoyed one of his films.

Many years ago, when Allen seemed intent on making ponderous paeans to Ingmar Bergman, I suggested he be strapped into a chair and forced to watch *Sullivan's Travels* until he got the message: There's no shame in being entertaining. *Melinda and Melinda,* is Woody Allen's meditation on this very subject.

The setup is simple: A group of friends are at dinner, when one starts to recount an incident. There are two playwrights present—one an author of dramas, the other of comedies. In the incident, which involves a woman named Melinda, each sees potential grist for their mill—the movie plays out both scenarios.

In typical Woody Allen fashion, this takes place in good restaurants and well-appointed New York apartments. In the end, we are left to consider how often the events in our lives can be cast as a tragedy or a comedy—it all depends on how you look at it, and how you tell the story.

Many critics have already weighed in on *Melinda and Melinda,* and found it wanting. Yet I, despite a few awkward moments of dialogue and acting (the inevitable Woody Allen neurotic imitation), found myself charmed. Allen is working in a Lubitsch mode, using Vilmos Zsigmond as his cinematographer to create a warm palette, an intimate world where ambition, love and betrayal intersect.

After the screening, I went home and looked up Allen's film credits. In my mind, Allen hadn't made a good film since *Annie Hall* and *Manhattan.* But reviewing his oeuvre to date, I was surprised by how many of his more recent films I had liked: Some, like *Hannah and Her Sisters, Zelig,* and *Broadway Danny Rose* were quite good; others, such as *Bullets Over Broadway* and *Mighty Aphrodite* and the underrated *Manhattan Murder Mystery,* may have been slight, but they were fun, and others still, like *Crimes and Misdemeanors* and *Deconstructing Harry,* could pass for great. Even *Sweet and Lowdown* was buoyed by great performances by Sean Penn and Samantha Morton. On the other hand, *Small Time Crooks, Curse of the Jade Scorpion* and *Celebrity* were films so odiferous they seemed to indicate a nadir. Still, in light of all the good work, I wondered: Why was I fixated on the stinkers? Why did a new Woody Allen film no longer feel like an important cultural event? What exactly was my Woody Allen problem?

Maybe it's hard for any moviemaker to remain relevant over a forty-year career. But in Allen's case, part of the problem—it goes without saying—has to do with the Woodman himself.

At the beginning of his career, Allen created a character, an underdog, that everyone could root for. He wasn't handsome, he had glasses and stringy hair, he wasn't strong or athletic, he was neurotic in the extreme, and nervous and clumsy in both action and his way of speaking. And he had trouble getting a date (most famously in *Annie Hall*, when he failed at picking up a girl who was planning to commit suicide the next night). But he was smart, wily, charming and his aggressive anger at his betters was strangely endearing. In the end, in his movies, he got the girl and then had to decide if he really wanted what he had got. In a young Woody Allen this was appealing.

However, as we watch ourselves and our fellow travelers age, behavior that appears charming in our twenties or even early thirties can seem pathological and disturbing in someone in their late thirties, forties, or fifties. With Allen, there was always a gap between his on-screen persona and his self.

In reality, Allen was no ninety-eight pound weakling—he was a good athlete, a rabid sports fan, an autodidact who lived on the Upper East Side, wore fine clothes and was politically more nuanced than his films would lead you to believe. As for his private life, he seemed to have serial monogamy down pat—until all hell broke loose with l'affaire Soon-Yi.

Once Allen's private life became public, and sordid details and allegations filled the air like confetti on New Year's Eve, it was no longer possible to see him on screen and suspend disbelief. His defense—that he was following his heart—did not make him more appealing.

And he had another problem: He was getting older. Harrison Ford and Michael Douglas may date women half their age, but most viewers are uncomfortable seeing older men on screen in romantic scenes. Just as after a certain age, the face looking back in the mirror is not the one we see when we close our eyes, so, too, we prefer our romantic film leads to stay, in the words of the Bobster, forever young.

This put Allen in a bind: If he appeared in a romantic role, viewers became uncomfortable; however, if he cast a young actor to substitute for the "Woody Allen" character, such as Jason Biggs, the performance inevitably foundered. Woody wrote for Woody, and no one, it seemed, could play him, even himself.

Many years ago, I found myself at Michael's Pub in New York watching Woody Allen playing clarinet with his Dixieland jazz band. As the band was about to break, I made my way to the men's room. I was standing at the urinal, when suddenly, I noticed that someone was standing next to me. It was Woody Allen.

We had a moment where we locked eyes, and I said, "How's it going?" Trust me, all I expected was a head nod, if that.

Instead, Allen launched into a short diatribe—explaining that doing something over and over again on the same night was sometimes more about compulsion than enjoyment. "It's not as much fun as it looks," he concluded.

For the last forty years, Woody Allen has made one or two films a year—usually identified as "Woody Allen Fall Project" or "Woody Allen Spring Project." I think we can surmise that the making of these movies has, at times, involved more compulsion than enjoyment

But sometimes if you do something long enough, you get a second wind. Look at the career of Phillip Roth. Or Dylan, who claims in his recent *Chronicles* that after decades of being lost, he once again found a way to play his music and create his sound. And with *Melinda and Melinda,* it seems Allen has found his way back to filmmaking.

As for Allen himself, turns out Soon-Yi Previn was not Lolita. Turns out she's Oona O'Neil (as in Charlie Chaplin's last wife), the woman who domesticated him, made him a family and a family man. (And if you want to see how Soon-Yi kicks his butt, just watch the documentary *Wild Man Blues.*) Allen knows: Things can change, even for those most set in their ways.

Woody Allen will turn seventy this year. He has made a film that asks: Who is responsible for the drama, the disappointment in our lives; who is responsible for the happiness? Is it just a matter of how we tell the story?

In *Melinda and Melinda,* the Woodman is back.

March 24, 2005

LUCK OF THE EXILES

Spring is upon us. My allergies have been acting up for weeks. So it seems the right time to talk about cross-pollination, a subject that it is at the heart of important new exhibits in Los Angeles and New York.

When Massachusetts Gov. Michael Dukakis was running for president in 1988, he often talked about his father, a Greek immigrant who had come to this country with no money, had worked very hard and made a considerable fortune. When he was young, Dukakis assumed that by working hard everyone could do the same. Then, one day, he realized that his father was not like everyone else. His father had chosen to come to this country specifically to get an education. His father was motivated to make a better life. And his father had certain abilities that not every one had. In fact, Dukakis was convinced that had you dropped his father into any country—or even on the moon—he would have become a business success. That was certainly true for my father as well.

This came to mind last Sunday when I visited the Skirball Cultural Center's exhibit *Driven Into Paradise* about Los Angeles' European Jewish émigrés of the 1930s and 1940s (the exhibit runs through May 8). This fascinating exhibit, organized by Tal Gozani, the Skirball's associate curator, chronicles the experiences of 10 cultural figures who came to Los Angeles, including composers Ernest Toch and Arnold Schoenberg; writers Vicki Baum (*Grand Hotel*), Lion Feuchtwanger (*Jud Suss*), Franz Werfel (*The Song of Bernadette*) and Salka Viertel (*Queen Christina*); ceramacist Otto Natzler and his wife, Gertrud; and art promoter Emilie "Galka" Scheyer.

I was a consultant on the Billy Wilder and Michael Curtiz installations, so I am biased, but the exhibit does a great job at showing how these individuals adapted to America and how America adapted to them. I went into the exhibit thinking: How lucky they were to escape Germany/Austria/Hungary! But seeing the exhibit, what became obvious is that these highly talented, highly motivated individuals made their own luck. They all saw the writing on the wall and, unlike many others, they not only could read that writing, they acted upon it. These émigrés were bound to be successful wherever they landed. Wilder and Curtiz, it is clear, would have found their way to Hollywood, one way or another.

Otto Natzler influenced a generation of ceramicists, making an art of what had been a craft in this country. Scheyer introduced the paintings of Kadinsky, Klee and Feininger to the United States (her collection is now part of the Norton Simon in Pasadena). Try to imagine our cultural heritage bereft of *Casablanca* or *Some Like It Hot, Song of Bernadette* or *Grand Hotel.* It certainly would have been our loss.

Viertel is also featured prominently in "*The Power of Conversation: Jewish Women and their Salons*" (at The Jewish Museum in New York through July 10). Curated by Emily Bilsky, the show is a fascinating exhibit on 14 influential Jewish women from the 18th, 19th and 20th century who created salons where people of different classes and artists of all stripes, could sponsor, discuss and support new art and social change. Henriette Herz and Rahel Varhagen's salons in 1780s Berlin nurtured the new romantic movement, while Fanny Mendelsohn's music salon welcomed Nicola Paganini, Clara Schumann and also premiered new works including her own compositions. Genevieve Straus in Paris was the close friend and inspiration of Marcel Proust (she was the model for the Duchess de Guermantes), while Gertrude Stein launched modernism in her salon (imagine being in the room when Stein said, "Picasso, meet Matisse"). Viertel is featured as the last salonist, and the only one in America, her Santa Monica home the locus where Bertol Brecht could mingle with the Great Garbo, Thomas Mann and Eisenstein on the beach.

What comes through loud and clear is that art does not occur in a vacuum. Lives were being led, and the places and people they interacted with are part of the story of how culture occurs.

Los Angeles is often characterized as paradise or purgatory—the place of exile. A 1999 book edited by Paul Vangelisti with Evan Calbi, *LA Exile: A Guide To Los Angeles Writing 1932-1998* (Marsilio, 1999), catalogues writers and artists who graced our shores—from Theodor Adorno, who spent a great deal of time here from 1938-1948, to Tennessee Williams, who living in Santa Monica in 1943, got fired from writing a movie for Lana Turner and used his savings to complete a play he was writing, later to be titled *The Glass Menagerie.*

The legacy of Feuchtwanger as exile, humanitarian and as salon host lives on in the work of the Villa Aurora Foundation.

Each year they award a fellowship for up to 12 months to a writer who is being persecuted or forced to live in exile. On March 22, at Feuchtwanger's former home in Pacific Palisades, The Villa Aurora, the foundation held a welcoming evening for this year's fellow, Syl Cheney-Coker, a poet and novelist from Sierra Leone.

Los Angeles is vast and spread out—we all relish the splendid isolation the city affords us, but it is also something we must struggle with. Los Angeles has incubated a few political salons, but where are the music, the writing, the art salons? Certainly guilds and professional organizations, as well as museums and cultural institutions, try to host them. But if history is any indication, it is the will of one person that will determine where the next Picasso meets the next Matisse; where we first hear the works of the next Mendelsohn; and where the Marcel Proust of Hancock Park will find his muse

April 10, 2005

LEAVING LA

When I go out of town, I often take a novel or two with me, knowing that a plane ride remains one of the few places to get serious reading done. Recently, I read two novels, Seth Greenland's *The Bones* (Bloomsbury) and Bruce Bauman's *And the Word Was* (Other Press), which made strong impressions about why, every so often, you need to get out of town. Both novels concern characters who believe their lives are at a dead end, and who leave their homes for experiences that, in the end, allow them to return to a life less examined but worth living.

Greenland's *The Bones,* although revolving around the lives of a downwardly spiraling stand-up comic and an upwardly mobile sitcom writer, is not so much a Hollywood novel as it is a novel about frustration, contempt, social and artistic ambition, talent (or the lack thereof); how they play out in our lives, and what it is one set of characters must do to exorcize the self-images that have come to define them. So it stands to reason that my own friendship with Seth and envy of his novel's success (rave reviews in The New York Times and Entertainment Weekly, movie option by John Calley at Sony for David Mamet, etc.) should keep me from writing about *The Bones*—but it won't:

Frank Bones, a brilliant, dark stand-up comic, a genius of self-destruction, has been cast as an Eskimo in a TV pilot. Lloyd Melnick, a former journalist for a New York alternative weekly who wrote a feature on Frank and crashed for a brief moment on his couch, is now a hugely well-paid sitcom writer with a resentment-inspiring development deal, all by virtue of having been on the writing staff of *The Fleishman Show* (a Seinfeld-like phenomenon), a show whose co-creator wrote every episode.

Melnick finds himself trapped in a life and a lifestyle he never wanted. At the same time, Frank Bones has been "The Bones" for so long he has never paused to think beyond the next pain-dulling pleasure or put-down. They both look to the other for their salvation. Melnick feels he can redeem his sitcom work by writing a novel—or a book—about Frank. Frank begs Melnick to write a pilot with him, or at least punch-up the Eskimo show. Instead they end up together in Tulsa, Okla., and on the run in Mexico.

Greenland's Los Angeles will be familiar to all who inhabit the Westside—and compelling to all who don't. It is tempting to play "guess who?" with characters, events, places, companies and organizations—but that is a distraction from Greenland's prose stylings—the finely wrought sentences, the razor-sharp puns and references, the laugh-out-loud absurdities captured by his unerring eye and the unrelenting rhythm that animates the story. *The Bones* is a literary novel that takes its humor seriously, but is funny about the absurdities of present LA modern life.

In LA author Bruce Bauman's *And the Word Was,* Dr. Neil Downs, who describes himself simply as "a Jew," flees New York for India and work as resident physician for the U.S. Embassy in New Delhi. He leaves behind his wife and the aftermath of a high school shooting in which his son was murdered.

In New Delhi, Neil seeks out Levi Furtstenblum, an aged Holocaust survivor, a writer and philosopher (think Primo Levi meets Jacques Monod) to ask how one goes on living. At the same time he meets the intelligent and beautiful Indian activist Holika, who draws him into her prominent and wealthy Indian family's soap opera—their personal, political, financial and even medical conflicts and dramas.

The sights and smells of India, and the customs of the cross-section of people Neil meets, are rendered so convincingly that you will come to think you've lived in India as well. Neil's spiritual journey and how he finds his way back to his wife, his home, and to his own sense of self, makes "And the Word Was" as rewarding in parts as it is intellectually challenging in others.

In both *The Bones* and *And the Word Was,* the main characters go to extremes, and push themselves to transgress their way beyond their own comfort zones, all in order to feel capable of leading the lives they led before.

Why do these authors feel the need to have their characters leave town? There is more going on here than simple wanderlust or the eternal quest of the wandering Jew. Is it simply a matter of shattering the illusion of stasis that Los Angeles' beautiful weather breeds? Or is it the desperation of no escape from our lives, even in the face of, in one case disaster, or in the other success? Which of us could ever board "that midnight train to Georgia" with our heads held high? Who could live with the epitaph: "Superstar, but he didn't get far"?

Perhaps we need look at this in context. The story of a character who leaves his home, journeys to a foreign place, and then returns to his home and to his wife a wiser, humbler man is an odyssey that has been told as long as—well, since Homer recounted *The Odyssey* itself. The journey is not, in of itself, the path to self-knowledge.

Sometimes leaving LA is the only way to realize what you're missing.

April 21, 2005

RAYMOND'S END

A Visit with the Deli Lama

Phil Rosenthal, the creator of *Everybody Loves Raymond,* which will end its nine-year run on CBS on May 16, and I are fressing at Barney Greengrass in Beverly Hills high atop Barney's Department Store. It's not that eating sable is the way I mourn (how is it that a fish can be named after a fur coat my mother owned?)—or that toasted bagels and cream cheese dulls the imminent loss of my favorite sitcom.

The reason is altogether different: I used to frequent a deli on Manhattan's Upper East Side called P.J. Bernstein's. In high school it had been a favorite haunt of young ladies from the Lenox School to whom I will be forever grateful for teaching me the invaluable phrase "scooped-out bagel." After college, as I began my adult life in New York, I would drop in occasionally for some sustenance. P.J. Bernstein's had a certain grungy charm, excellent brisket, tasty hamburgers and an eccentric staff.

Turns out I should have been nicer to the maitre d'. During 1981-82, Rosenthal was the maitre d', the manager—he ran the show. The owner, in Rosenthal's words "a very nice alcoholic," would wait for Rosenthal's arrival at 3 p.m. Rosenthal's job was to make him a vodka, then another, then another—and after three drinks he would leave the restaurant to Rosenthal's care telling him "to eat what he wanted and take what he wanted." It was there, at the deli, that Rosenthal learned everything he would one day need to know to run a successful sitcom.

Rosenthal had graduated from Hofstra University with the ambition of being an actor. Accordingly, he got a job as a guard at the Metropolitan Museum of Art. He often worked the graveyard shift. With the museum to himself, Rosenthal would turn on the lights and study paintings much closer than any visitor would be allowed. Van Gogh's works touched him and he returned the compliment. But his continuing-ed program in art history ended when Rosenthal was found asleep during his shift in a 300-year-old bed. A friend had recently left his job at P.J. Bernstein's and recommended Rosenthal. Helping himself to the food made him a not-so-starving actor. "I loved it."

Here's what he learned at P.J. Bernstein: "It's not so different from running a show. You're in charge of everything. Every single decision is made by you. First of all, you're financially responsible. Next, you're creatively responsible because of running the thing. Thirdly, everybody is coming to you with their problems: the waitresses hate each other; the countermen hate each other—they're not talking. The customers are mad about a sandwich. You have to handle all this. You're juggling many things. That's the main comparison."

Also, he learned how to cater to stars (literally and figuratively) as when Howard Cosell would walk in and in one breath say, "Hello Philip, I'll have a vodka on the rocks; join me."

Rosenthal was still trying to be an actor when Alan

Kirschenbaum, a friend of his from high school, appeared at his apartment carrying a new-fangled machine, a word processor, and suggested that he and Rosenthal write a script. They wrote a story about their hometown and a suburban detective and sold the script to HBO Films. Although it never got made, Rosenthal got paid $75,000, a sum that both impressed and, Rosenthal suspects, annoyed his mother.

Within a few years Rosenthal found himself and his writing partner, Oliver Goldstick, working on a number of ill-fated TV shows such as the Robert Mitchum sitcom, *A Family for Joe* (1990); the Ray Sharkey sitcom, *The Man in the Family* (1991); the *Look Who's Talking* spinoff, *Baby Talk* (1991-92), and Alan Kirschenbaum's early Fox Channel confection, *Down the Shore* (1992-93). Rosenthal graduated to being a supervising producer on *Coach,* but having parted ways amicably with his writing partner, Rosenthal was open to offers.

Rosenthal was sent a tape of a young comic, Ray Romano. As the tape began, Rosenthal realized he had seen this performance by Romano on Letterman and it had made him laugh. Romano was talking about his kids. "His stuff was so relatable," Rosenthal now says, "it reminded me of a young Bill Cosby—and that's where I live." Based on that six-minute performance, Letterman had said this guy should have a show. Rosenthal was interested.

Romano and Rosenthal met at Art's Deli in Studio City. They hit it off. They were both from Queens, and both had families who were, in Rosenthal's words, "Somewhat intrusive." "For every story about his facacta family," Rosenthal said, "I had one too." Rosenthal got the job.

Romano was a fan of Seinfeld and thought that his show, too, should be Ray and his friends in the coffee shop riffing on current events. "I said I can't do that show," Rosenthal said, "I'm not that guy."

Rosenthal said that he loved Ray's stand-up act and the show should be based on that—his kids and his wife. Then Rosenthal said the fateful words: "Tell me about the rest of your family."

"He tells me," Rosenthal recalled, "he's got twin boys and an older daughter and his parents live close by and they're always over. And his dad's a little crazy and he has an older brother who's a New York police sergeant who's divorced who lives with his parents and touches every bite of food to his chin and whenever he sees Ray get another accomplishment, he says, 'It never ends for Raymond....Everybody loves Raymond.'"

"That's the show!" Rosenthal said.

"That's not a show," Romano said.

"That's a show," Rosenthal said.

Rosenthal knew Romano had never acted before. So it made sense to have him play a character that was close to his stage persona. "Plus," Rosenthal said, "I could relate to it. What I didn't know about his family, I could fill in with the characters in my family."

I asked Rosenthal to tell me about the characters in his family. His answer: "You see them every week on 'Everybody loves Raymond.'"

Both Rosenthal's parents were born in Germany. His father's family left after Kristallnacht. His mother and her mother did not. They were separated from her father and managed to escape to France and from there to a ship bound for the United States. The ship was turned away and Rosenthal's mother and grandmother spent two years in Cuba before arriving in New York. They later learned that Rosenthal's maternal grandfather survived Auschwitz. After the war, he remained in Germany to work for the Bavarian Reparations Committee, but died before Rosenthal was born.

Many writers, including this correspondent, have discussed the Barone family dynamics as being fundamentally Jewish and have pegged the show's extreme dark humor that borders on the cruel as the sine qua non of Holocaust survivor families. The popularity of *Raymond,* I once argued, is assimilation in the best sense of the word—that is of Jewish values and sensibility absorbed into American culture (as opposed to the reverse).

Rosenthal knew he was onto something when he started getting reaction to the pilot where Ray gives his mother a gift from the "Fruit of the Month Club." Would you be surprised to hear that story was true, based on Rosenthal's mother. "She reacted as if I had sent her plutonium."

"I thought people would find it quirky and funny." What Rosenthal didn't expect is that everyone would think it was about their own family. From that he learned an important lesson: "The more specific you are in the writing, the more universal it is."

Today *Raymond* appears in 141 countries and the show gets mail from families over all the world who feel that their own stories are appearing on screen.

To his parents who once chastised Rosenthal for watching too much TV asking, "What are you going to do? Get a job watching TV?" Rosenthal sent a big-screen TV with a note saying, "Ha, Ha."

Perhaps somewhere there is a support group for men whose mothers loved them too much, and whose mother's intensity was only matched by their father's remoteness; for children who loved their parents even though they were annoying, meddling and favored them and their accomplishments over their sibling. I don't know about you but mine met every Monday at 9 p.m. That is the specific.

As for the universal: *Raymond* appeals to people everywhere because it reassured us that all the conflict, ill feeling, cruelty and bad behavior that occurs within a family is nonetheless done in the name of love. Rosenthal's genius, his gift, was to transform these feelings which usually simmer within us unresolved, or break families apart, into humor—side-splitting humor.

Everyone has favorite episodes: Among Rosenthal's favorites is the show that explains how Ray and Debra met, which Rosenthal and Romano wrote together; also the "Italy" show; the "Baggage" episode where Ray and Debra's fight over who will put away a suitcase; and many, many more. Mine include those as well as the episode where Ray's mother intercedes with the FBI regarding a job Ray's brother has applied for; and the "Container" that notably includes a spoof on Hitchcock.

Soon after the show began, Rosenthal got offers to develop other shows. He decided that doing so would be a mistake. He looked around and observed that in most cases, the original show suffered and the new show failed to be as good. Rosenthal not only decided to stay at *Raymond,* he even gave Disney back their development deal money.

He realized how rare it was to have a hit show. And he was writing about his family. When would that happen again? So he decided he would do the show until he couldn't anymore; until he had run out of good ideas. The question then became how long could that go on for? Rosenthal as a student of the sitcom form, conducted his own study. "Mary Tyler Moore," a "near-perfect show" in Rosenthal's estimation, lasted seven seasons. Seven became the number. However, during *Raymond*'s seventh season the staff found they had enough stories for an eighth season. And Rosenthal intended that to be their last. But in the middle of season eight, people were clamoring for a ninth. Rosenthal knew everyone was having a ball, no one wanted it to end, but he felt he had to be adult, or as he said: "I have to run the deli."

Although he had said "no way," he asked the writers to meet in January to see if they had any stories that were good enough for a ninth season. Rosenthal found they had six. He figured that meant they could reasonably do twelve. He told CBS, they were ecstatic. They said, could you do eighteen? He said, thirteen, they said, seventeen, he said fifteen, they said sixteen—he said—sold! And that's how the ninth season came to have 16 episodes ending on Monday, May 16, 2005.

Meanwhile back at Barney Greengrass, Phil Rosenthal was not sure what the future would bring. He was taking a vacation with his family, and then hoped to catch up on his sleep before seeing what he would write next. As for me, I was taking no chances this time. With the maitre d' looking on, I tipped generously.

May 5, 2005

LIGHT OF DAY

As I drove toward Malibu the other day, Santa Monica Bay was anything but uniform, a shifting collage of textures and hues of blue. As the sun glinted off the water, I wondered: How does one describe the special quality of Santa Monica light? How do you explain it? How do you quantify it?

To find the answer, I went to the new Robert Weingarten photo exhibit, *6:30 am,* which runs through July 17 at the Frederick R. Weisman Museum of Art at Pepperdine University in Malibu.

Over a year, beginning in January 2003, Weingarten shot the same view from his Malibu home over Santa Monica Bay, at the same time of day, capturing the light and the vista in an incredible variety of colors and impressions. The result challenges the very assumption of how and what we see.

That *6:30 am,* is both set in Malibu and exhibited there is serendipity. Yet the connection between Weingarten, Weisman, the museum and Malibu itself, all of which meet at the intersection of art and commerce, Jewish ambition and desire, between what we do and how we live, what we look at and what we see, seems strangely congruent.

The Weisman Museum was founded in 1992 by Frederick Weisman (1912-1994), a Minneapolis-born businessman whose passion for collecting and exhibiting art, when paired with that of his family's, has been a driving force behind LA's modern art institutions. Norton Simon, of Pasadena museum fame, was his brother-in-law. His first wife, Marcia, was instrumental in building the modern art collections at LACMA and founding MOCA. Weisman was active in LACMA and MOCA and also launched the art collection at Cedars-Sinai.

According to Michael Zakian its director, the Weisman Museum focuses on California art since 1960, exhibiting artists who play an important role in the contemporary scene. Recent shows of note include painter Wayne Thibaud and glass artist Dale Chihuly.

Once a year, the museum hosts a show of works curated from Weisman's art foundation. That Weisman's passion for art overtook his life of commerce makes showing the work of Weingarten at the Weisman Museum unusually appropriate.

Weingarten was born in Brooklyn in 1941 and graduated from Baruch College with a degree in finance. He had a passion for photography, but like many a "good Jewish boy," chose the business world over the art world. Working on Wall Street in insurance and international reinsurance he became wealthy. In 1983, he moved to Los Angeles.

"I got sick of New York," he says. In Los Angeles he continued his business activities and became culturally and philanthropically involved as president and chairman of the board of the LA Philharmonic.

Weingarten had not lost his passion for photography, but neither had he pursued it as seriously as he wanted. In his early

50s, Weingarten decided it had to become the dominant activity in his life. He took a series of master classes with photographers such as Charlie Waite, whom Weingarten calls "the Ansel Adams of England." When curators and collectors who had no idea who he was started buying and asking to exhibit Weingarten's work, he felt vindicated.

For the last seven years, Weingarten's photographs have appeared in over 50 exhibits, and are in the collection of several museums, including the Getty, the Santa Barbara Museum and the Whitney Museum in New York.

6:30 am came out of a challenge by Weston Naef, the Getty's photo curator, which follows Alfred Stieglitz's famous dictum that "no photographer should travel anywhere to find a picture if he cannot first find one close to home."

Although Weingarten mounted a 2 1/4-inch format camera on a tripod and shot the same view every morning at 6:30 a.m., creating certain constants, Weingarten found aesthetic decisions in his choices of lens, f-stops and how much sky and how much water to feature (70/30), as well as in the printing process.

As with Monet's paintings of haystacks, Weingarten sought, in his words, "to prove chromatic adaptation," that is, to show the gap between what colors exist and what our brain tells us is there. It's the difference, Weingarten said recently, "between looking and seeing."

The resulting images speak like paintings to a wide range of references, from Monet to Turner's sunsets to Rothko-like color fields. They are beautiful and scary, and as we are wont to say in LA, "awesome." One would never have imagined such a wide range of colors and effects possible in Southern California, the place derided for having no seasons and for every day being the same. On a deeper level, that is exactly his point.

When Freud discussed "repetition compulsion" in "Beyond the Pleasure Principle," he acknowledged that we repeat actions that are essentially painful, re-experiencing the trauma and anxieties produced in a Sisyphean cycle. Yet, viewing Weingarten's exhibit put me in mind of other fixed compulsions, or rather devotions. I thought of attending the morning prayers to say Kaddish during the year of mourning for my father.

I thought about the cycle of a daily run or the morning routine of my daughter before she goes to school. When I think of each, I recall a single experience and regard the whole as one day repeated over and over. Yet, if I really reflect on the pictures in my mind, radical differences emerge.

The beauty of Weingarten's *6:30 am,* exists not only in the images he has captured. He reminds us that no two days are the same.

May 19, 2005

AGENTS OF CHARITY

As I write this The Jewish Family Service (JFS) of Los Angeles' annual gala to be held on June 1, 2005 is a few days away. The honorees are CAA agent Rick Kurtzman; his brother, Fox business affairs executive Howard Kurtzman; and their brother-in-law, William Morris Agent David Lonner (married to their sister Janet).

JFS is a wonderful and important organization that, since 1854, has provided mental health and social services to men, women and children of all faiths and ethnicities.

The Kurtzmans in all their extended glory are a great family. Our connection is through Rick and Wendy Kurtzman and through our daughters. My friendship with Rick is such that we recently saw *Star Wars Episode III: Revenge of the Sith* together. For men, that's about as close as it gets.

By the time this column appears the event will already be past. I trust many of you attended and many more contributed; and for those who didn't it's not too late (see www.jfsla.org; they'd be happy to accept a contribution, even now). But I thought I would use this occasion to discuss something completely different: Hollywood, Jews, ethics and morals.

As a rule, agents are not held in high moral esteem by either Hollywood denizens or the public at large (that is, the readers of

Vanity Fair and gossip columns). Michael Ovitz's fall and subsequent drumming in the press have not added luster to the profession. As Lady Caroline Lamb said, when asked about the morals of Lord Byron: "It's the first I've heard of them."

Being an agent is fraught with apparent conflicts: How do you lobby for one client rather than another? How do you sign a client who already has an agent (less politely called poaching)—even if you could better serve that client? At every turn, in every deal, opportunities abound to lie and misrepresent the truth.

Although agents are subject to state regulation, enforcement is lax, to say the least.

And agents do, on occasion, behave intolerably. Some have even stolen from their agency or clients. But with rare exception, as when *Desperate Housewives* creator Marc Cherry discovered that his agent, Marcie Wright, was embezzling from him, agents do not get turned over to police or even sued. More often than not, the agency dismisses them with a generous settlement and an even more generous press release. Agencies are disinclined to institute a criminal or civil suit that would open the agency's books and business to prying eyes.

Hollywood's long history of Jewish employment begs an interesting question: To what extent are Jewish agents, or indeed the profession itself, informed by Judaism or held accountable to some form of Jewish moral standard.

A recent New Yorker profile of William Morris President David Wirtschafter caused a sensation, particularly when some of his named clients left him post-publication. Wirtschafter's misstep may have been telling the truth—out loud and in print. That may not seem a sin, but as the Talmud tells us, sometimes not holding your tongue is the worse thing one can do.

All told, I have never been convinced that the morals of agents, or the moral dilemmas of those in the agency business, differ from any other profession. Consider real estate, the art world, Wall Street—all have their share of scoundrels, beloved and reviled.

Morals and ethics reside within the person, not the profession. Further, there is a difference between ethics and morals. Ethics are of the moment; morals are of a higher, more permanent order. (Which is why no one ever talks about "situational morals.")

It follows that there are many kinds of agents (and I don't mean Orthodox, Conservative and Reform). Some are young heat-seeking missiles on the move, networking their way to studio or production-company jobs. Others are salespersons, with little depth, but great enthusiasm—and they are all about the sale. Others are more entrepreneurial and are about building the business of their agency and/or creating business opportunities for their clients and themselves.

A very few number—and in these I include Rick Kurtzman and David Lonner—value and exude professionalism. Although very competitive, they are all about the people they represent—about standing by them and doing the hard work. They see that as their job; the rest does not interest them.

When I asked Kurtzman about the ethical and moral conflicts he encounters, he said, "I never put myself in a position where I have those problems." That may sound simplistic. But it's as simple as that. Sometimes morals are as much about what we don't do, as about what we do.

Which brings me to the annual gala of Jewish Family Service of Los Angeles. So what does it mean to be honored by an important and venerable charity?

It is not so much an award as an agreement. In most cases, it means that you are willing to make calls for the charity and have your PDA contacts exploited, as well as your friends, family and business associates, all in the service of fundraising for this charity evening.

If that sounds like a hassle, it is.

So why do it? Why did Rick, Howard and David agree to be honored?

The answer is simple: Because these honorees grew up learning the meaning of tzedakah, or acts of charity and lovingkindness.

Lynette Kurtzman, Howard and Rick's mother, is a longtime JFS board member who co-chaired the 1999 JFS gala; their father, Ray Kurtzman, one of the original pillars of CAA, served on the boards of the Jewish Community Foundation and The Jewish Federation of Greater Los Angeles. David recalls his own father being honored by the United Jewish Appeal. Philanthropy was passed from generation to generation.

Tzedakah, according to some commentators, is the most important Jewish commandment; as important as all the others combined. It is also, according to Yom Kippur liturgy, one of three acts that can absolve us of our sins.

That should come as good news to at least some of the agents in the room at the JFS event.

June 2, 2005

HEART TO HART

A few weeks ago, the Getty Playhouse showcased a memorable special event: "Here's to Life," Kitty Carlisle Hart's cabaret-style, one-woman show, accompanied by her musical director, David Lewis.

Hart, ninety-four, performed for a little over an hour, reminiscing and singing songs from some of her late friends such as Jerome Kern, George Gershwin, Richard Rogers, Oscar Hammerstein II and Cole Porter, presenting in one evening a short history of the American musical theater.

My daughter, who is 7, knows Kitty Carlisle as the star of the Marx Brothers' *A Night at the Opera.* I recall her as a panelist on *To Tell the Truth.*

In 1998, Hart, who had recently published her autobiography *Kitty,* was asked to give a lecture on the American musical theater.

"What would I say?" Hart recalled asking.

She was told: "Just talk about the giants of the theater. You've known them all."

Instead of lecturing, she put together a show where she sings their songs and tells tales of them. She's been performing the show periodically ever since.

She looks great on stage, making all the sixty- and seventy-year-olds in the audience feel young—and making those even younger feel that one can indeed stop time. Hart told the audience that she's still got great legs—and then proved it.

She was born Catherine Conn (pronounced Cohen) in New Orleans. Her father was a doctor; her mother, Hortense, was the daughter of Benjamin Holzman, Shreveport's first elected Jewish mayor. There's an anecdote about her mother's desire to assimilate being so great that once, when a taxi driver asked if her daughter was Jewish, Hortense answered: "She may be, but I'm not."

Hart's father died when she was ten. The next year, she decamped with her mother to Europe—where over the next several years Hart studied in Switzerland, at the Sorbonne in Paris and at the London School of Economics and the Royal Academy of Dramatic Art in London.

Her mother had hoped to marry her off to European royalty. They returned to New York, without success, where her mother allowed Kitty to pursue a stage career. She appeared in several musicals and operettas before being summoned to Hollywood.

Hart recalled that it was on the set of *A Night at the Opera,* with The Marx Brothers, or as she called them "those knock-about boys" that George Kaufman introduced her to his former writing partner Moss Hart. At the time he didn't pay much attention to her.

But George Gershwin, whom she had met in New York, did. He was something of a ladies' man and she recalled that Gershwin had a little waltz that he would pretend to have composed on the spot for whichever woman he was wooing. Gershwin even invited her to a seder at his mother's house, where Oscar

Levant presided and Gershwin delivered a jazz version of the haggadah.

It would take another six years before she sat before Hart at a New York party and said to him the words he most wanted to hear, "Tell me about your trip to the South Pacific." She became his best audience. They were married in 1941 and had two children (her son, Chris Hart, directed the recent production of *You Can't Take It With You* at the Geffen).

Moss Hart was the first playwright to win the Pulitzer Prize, for *You Can't Take it With You* in 1936. He's also remembered for *The Man Who Came To Dinner,* the libretto for *Lady in the Dark,* the screenplay for *Gentleman's Agreement* and for directing the Broadway productions of *My Fair Lady* and *Camelot.* He died in 1961.

As Kitty Carlisle Hart sang Gershwin's *The Man I Love* and Rogers and Hammerstein's *Something Wonderful* from *The King and I,* and also songs from Jerome Kern, Irving Berlin and Arthur Schwartz, I thought about the amazing impact her circle had on American musical theater.

I was reminded, too, of the late Marlon Brando, who told Larry King, "If it weren't for the Jews, we wouldn't have, oddly enough, Broadway and Tin Pan Alley and all the standards that were written by Jews. All the songs you love to sing."

Brando was criticized for his remarks, but it highlights the influence of those close to Kitty Carlisle Hart.

There's a strand in the American musical theater that seems to trace its roots to a cantorial tradition. *The Jazz Singer,* the first talkie, had as its very premise the generational transition from performance within the synagogue to making it on the secular stage. Hart's circle of largely assimilated Jews were writing shows for and about America, musicals like *Show Boat, Oklahoma,* and *South Pacific.* Like the first Hollywood moguls, they were creating America in their own image. Their collective legacy is a fount of plays and musicals that continue to be revived on Broadway and the world over.

To see Kitty Carlisle Hart perform their canon is to be beguiled by her charm—and her vitality. After her performance at the Geffen, Hart played an engagement aboard a cruise ship for two weeks. She is booked to play at Feinstein's at the Regency Hotel in New York in September for her 95th Birthday.

Hart closed her performance at the Geffen with Artie Butler and Phyllis Molinari's *Here's to Life.* One can't help but remark: What a life it is.

June 30, 2005

HISTORY HAPPENS

After the intermission, the lights start to dim. A lone woman is on stage. She waits for the audience to settle in. She is well dressed, well groomed. She begins: "For the Palestinians, there is no other context. We see everything in the context of Palestine."

In the June 26 Los Angeles Times' Art Notes, Don Shirley reported that this speech draws the most intense reactions—applause and boos—of any scene in *Stuff Happens,* David Hare's play at the Mark Taper Forum about President Bush and Prime Minister Tony Blair's path to war in Iraq. (The title comes from Secretary of Defense Donald Rumsfeld's explanation of why looting occurred after the conquest of Baghdad.)

The woman who is described as "a Palestinian academic" in the published play version (Faber and Faber 2004) asks, "Why Iraq? Why now?" She explains that although there are many possible reasons for the war on Iraq—which she enumerates as "Arab democracy," "unfinished business" and "oil"—she says that for the Palestinians, "it's about one thing": Israel.

She goes on to wonder why Bush would enforce the U.N. resolutions against Iraq but not those against Israel. Why "terror is condemned, but state-sanctioned murder is green-lit."

She concludes that "the victims of the conflict have become the problem. We are the Jews of the Jews."

At the performance I attended on the Wednesday after the Times story, I noted one person murmuring "yeah" in agreement during the speech, no real boos (maybe one person saying "hold on, hold on") and there were some moments of applause—when she cited such reasons for war as Bush's dad, Vice President Dick Cheney and oil. Those moments of applause seemed no stronger or sustained than several others throughout the show.

Her speech lasts no more than a few minutes, if that. We never see her again. Her concerns are not really addressed by any other character; nor is there truly a dramatic payoff in the context of the rest of the play.

In the Times piece, Gordon Davidson, the play's director, said the speech "troubled me." However, he added that his feelings "don't necessarily have to be answered in the play." Davidson chose *Stuff Happens* as his final directorial effort, part of his artistic farewell after a decade as the Taper's artistic director.

Personally, I did not find the speech troubling. I thought it an accurate representation of an opinion that would have been expressed at the time. It is not the play's strongest moment—or its weakest. (The weakest is when a "Brit in New York" says, "On Sept. 11, America changed. Yes. It got much stupider.")

Nonetheless, let me list the reasons why *Stuff Happens* should be seen. (It runs through July 17.) First, you should see it as a work of drama. An incredibly deft and talented playwright has found a way to take the "stuff" of recent history—speeches, press conferences, reports by the participants—and shape these fragments, moments and documents into a narrative whose dramatic tension is only increased, because we know the end result.

You should see *Stuff Happens* regardless of personal politics for the way the characters are drawn and for the acting. Although we all have our own impressions of the main players—Bush, Cheney, Condoleezza Rice, Colin Powell, Rumsfeld and their English counterparts, Blair, Jack Straw and David Manning, as well as Hans Blix and Dominique de Villepin—seeing them onstage speaking their words, as we sit in the dark and listen again more closely, reveals new dimensions to their characters.

Finally, I would argue that you should see *Stuff Happens* because of the Palestinian academic's speech. Israel and the Middle East conflict is a minor but interesting subtheme of the play. Hare calls attention to Bush's support of Ariel Sharon and to Bush's disengagement from Yasser Arafat and the Palestinian authority. Hare also puts forward instances when Blair suggests that attention to the Middle East conflict would help him gain support in England for an Iraqi incursion.

The Palestinian academic is never heard of again after the opening of the second act. Deliberately or unconsciously, that speaks to a truth that few have ever acknowledged, and fewer still appreciate: Israel stands on firmer ground today than it did four years ago.

Consider that at the start of the millennium, with the Mideast peace process a failure, with President Bill Clinton and Israeli Prime Minister Ehud Barak out of office, with Bush and Sharon newly elected, Israel was facing an existential crisis. Intifida II was sending waves of suicide bombers into Israel.

At the same time, the vilification of Israel was becoming

loud and brazen, particularly in European and academic circles. A new anti-Semitism seemed to be infecting the world, of which the murder of Wall Street Journal reporter Daniel Pearl became a prominent example. For the first time in my own life—certainly for the first time since before the Six-Day War—there were questions about Israel's future.

Around that time, I remember attending an Israel Policy Forum breakfast at which Shimon Peres spoke. Someone asked him if there was any basis for hope. Peres replied, "There is always hope." He went on to say that if you had told a Jew in Poland in 1944 that in four years not only would the Nazis be defeated but that there would be a State of Israel, he would not have believed it possible.

After September 11, Bush's "war on terror" and in light of his claim that "either you are with us or you are with the terrorists,"one heard less and less support for suicide bombers and justification for attacks on the Israeli civilian population. Simply put, September 11 and the war in Iraq moved attacking Israel to the back burner, despite the attempts of persons such as Hare's "Palestinian academic" to link the United States and Israel in this matter.

Hare's play is worth seeing, because we deserve to understand how history happens. And there is no offense in the speech of the "Palestinian academic," because it reminds us that history cannot be hijacked by speeches. History occurs, for better or worse, in surprising ways. It is a reminder that "Stuff happens."

July 7, 2005

A WELL LIT PLACE

How does one create a literary community in Los Angeles? It is true that on any given night, there are readings, slams and events at bookstores, bars and auditoriums all over town. Yet rarely does this coalesce into a sense of community, a literary life in Los Angles.

Steve Wasserman, who is leaving the *LA Times* Sunday Book Review, tried to foster a community of books, of writers and of ideas in maximalist and minimalist ways, in the pages of the book review, with the *LA Times* Festival of Books and by helping establish the Los Angeles Institute of the Humanities at USC.

Wasserman spent his formative years in Berkeley, attending high school and UC Berkeley there. He arrived in Los Angeles in 1977 and worked at the LA Times from 1978 to 1984, rising to deputy editor of Sunday opinion and the op-ed page. He then did time in the New York book world before being offered, in 1996, "the only job for which I wouldn't have left" Los Angeles in the first place: editor of the Sunday Book Review.

"You have to beware in life," Wasserman said recently. "You sometimes get what you wish for."

His notion for the book section was simple: "I would pay

the readers of LA the respect [they were] long overdue. I would serve up book criticism in the language of adult..."

Los Angeles was "no longer the laid-back, insular province of yesteryear but rather a vast energetic megalopolis full of contradiction and complexity." It had become "a deeply neurotic, complicated place full of ambitious people..."

Moreover, Los Angeles is the country's second-largest bookselling market. *The New Yorker* magazine now has more subscribers in California than it does in New York; and The New York Review of Books has almost as many subscribers in California as it does in New York. These were facts worth leveraging.

The problem in Los Angeles, as Wasserman put it, was that "geography is fate." Los Angeles's vast, spread out freeway- and boulevard-linked archipelago has made, Wasserman observed, "whole communities invisible to each other."

In Los Angeles, he concluded, "Community is an act of will, not serendipity."

Wasserman sought to will the disparate voices of Los Angeles into a literary community.

The Festival of Books began prior to Wasserman's arrival, but he became its impresario, mixing serious writers and politics with a dash of Hollywood. Festival crowds reached 150,000 in 2003, according to the LA Times Media Center, demonstrating that Los Angeles' love of books is tangible.

Wasserman also launched the Los Angeles Institute for the Humanities with USC history department chair Steven Ross—a once-a-month luncheon speaker club of academics and artists: "Very selfishly, I wanted to be at a table with people much smarter than myself and share bad deli sandwiches."

As for The Sunday Book review itself, Wasserman found being editor an "inherently fraught" and "elusive" task. Given that the "local had gone global in LA a long time ago," Wasserman decided he would not review a writer just because he lived in 90210.

He would follow the advice Joan Didion gave him to "just review the good books." Those that were, in his words, "worthy of our readers."

Wasserman estimates that 150,000 books are published each year. The *LA Times* Sunday Book Review can feature around 1,200 (*The New York Times* Sunday Book Review reviews three times as many).

"My intention was to be three times as good in one-third the space," he said.

Wasserman's book section was criticized for being East Coast-centric and for reviewing too many books from obscure or academic presses. However, even detractors agree that he brought attention to works that otherwise would have been neglected.

Wasserman's proudest moment was a review by Octavio Paz of a new translation of the poetry of Sor Juana Ines de la Cruz, a 17th-century Mexican Carmelite nun. Sor Juana was unknown to most English-speaking readers—including Wasserman's employers. However as one of Mexico's greatest poets, cited as one of the great exemplars of both proto-feminist and Hispanic literature, it would be hard to argue her work was not relevant to Los Angeles' readers.

In the end, Wasserman said, "I had a pronounced set of convictions. I recognize that they were not shared by some."

Wasserman showcased the breadth and depth of intellectual

life in Los Angeles as well as its denizens' passion for books. He got the attention of editors, writers and publicists outside of Los Angeles, even outside of the United States by sending copies of the book review to a list of 2,000 literary luminaries (a perk *LA Times* management ended prior to Wasserman's resignation).

By the fall, there will be a new Sunday Book Review editor. That person will, in all probability, do what any person given the task usually does: feature larger type in certain places; assign book reviews to friends and writers they know and/or admire; and anoint new columnists to cover popular reading topics, be they mystery, science fiction, Hollywood or comics. In the end, the new manager will try to make the section his own or her own. Whether anyone will care or read it, or whether the reviews will sell books—for that, we will have to wait.

Wasserman has left the building, but his challenge remains: to nurture a literary community in Los Angeles, a metropolis that has yet to realize it has become the epicenter of 21st-century American creativity.

July 14, 2005

THE DREAM IS OVER

According to reports in various newspapers last week, NBC-Universal is contemplating acquiring Dream-Works' live-action feature-film division, or as it used to be called, their movie studio. Regardless of whether the acquisition is consummated, it reflects a sad truth: Steven Spielberg, Jeffrey Katzenberg and David Geffen's dream of creating a modern major studio has failed.

When Spielberg & Co. first announced the idea of creating a studio, more than a decade ago, before they had even chosen a company name, their vision included creating a state-of-the-art sound stage and production facility in Playa Vista. That was the first part to be jettisoned like some shuttle booster rocket as it ascended into space.

Next, there was talk about the studio as a creative entity—a place where "dream" projects would get made. United Artists, the company founded by Charlie Chaplin, Douglas Fairbanks and Mary Pickford was cited. But United Artists never fulfilled its creators' aspirations, nor did First Artists, a company created in the 1960s for more contemporary dreamers such as Dustin Hoffman.

I remember a meeting in which I took part shortly after DreamWorks launched, at the Southwestern-style offices that formerly had been Spielberg's production company, Amblin—or as I used to call it, The Adobe Disneyworld. Speilberg's Norman Rockwells were still on the walls of the hallway. The executive I met with, to whom I was pitching my own possible projects, has since moved on. But on this occasion, she told me about the freedom they had, and how they were open to all material "of quality." I left with no clear idea of what a "DreamWorks" movie was, and to this day I still can't say.

As for Spielberg, when he talked about creative freedom, I don't think most people understood that he was talking about the freedom to make most of his movies in partnerships with other studios. Katzenberg, who began at the top of the pyramid, quickly stepped off to become president of production, and then retreated to run the animation division. As for Geffen, I'm sure somebody knows what he does all day but it's not me (my best guess: makes phone calls). Geffen was apparently in charge of strategy of which we are now seeing the fruit.

DreamWorks was intended to be a modern creative hot house—an octopus with tentacles in any area the imagination might foster. That concept, however, falls well short of a viable business model.

DreamWorks launched one entity after another, including a game division that it later shuttered. And a television division it folded and a record label it also, in the end, jettisoned. As time went by, the company decided to focus on the core business: making movies—feature films and animated films.

These movies ran the gamut: good ones that made money, good ones that lost money and bad ones that made money. It was never precisely clear how much money, if any, DreamWorks was able to make. As I understand it, DreamWorks entered into many co-financing, and distribution deals, which make it more difficult to determine when the studio actually made a profit, especially one that would satisfy its investors.

Last fall, DreamWorks spun off its animation unit as a public company. Which meant that finally, billionaire investor Paul Allen could achieve some payback. But going public had other consequences.

For those who followed the Michael Eisner/Michael Ovitz imbroglio, you may recall that Eisner felt Ovitz didn't understand that behavior at a public company is different than at a private one.

Apparently that's a lesson that Katzenberg, who has toiled at several public companies, including Disney, forgot. Typical executive behavior—such as hyping upcoming releases or casting financial performance in a too-favorable light—can quickly become the focus of an investigation by the Securities and Exchange Commission (SEC). And the SEC is looking into DreamWorks Animation.

So why did the dream of creating a modern studio fail?

My theory of what happened begins by looking back to the early years of the industry in the first half of the 20th century. The original creators of the studio were, for the most part, Jewish immigrants possessed with a drive to make a living, filled with a hunger to make movies and also to make a profit. And they embodied, too, a desire to create institutions that survived them. They were dreamers pursuing their own "dreamworks." And they paid a price for their ambition—their wives, their children, their health suffered. But the studio came first. One can also argue this dynamic also applied to the more recent crop of moguls, such as Lew Wasserman and Rupert Murdoch.

By contrast, it is easy to imagine Spielberg or Geffen saying "Why do I need this hassle?"

They are too successful, too comfortable—they have full lives competing for their attention.

Katzenberg continues to work for the Dream, but it's more limited, and the longevity of his vision remains to be seen. DreamWorks seems fated to become a label at a studio, like New Line at Warner Bros. Perhaps one day the founders could say as Lord Byron did, "I had a dream which was not all a dream."

But today we mourn what could have been, even as we announce: Dream over.

August 4, 2005

A READ ON LIFE

Lately, I've been thinking about two novels I recently enjoyed: *The Other Shulman* by Alan Zweibel (Villard, $23.95), and *Joy Comes in the Morning* by Jonathan Rosen (Picador, $14).

The two novels are strikingly different: One deals with confronting a marriage of long standing; the other is about getting married. One is comic with serious moments; the other serious with comic moments. Yet both feature protagonists trying to decide whether they are running toward something, or away from it.

Shulman is the tale of a middle-aged New Jersey stationery store owner. Married for more than twenty years, with three kids out of the house, he's stuck, personally and professionally, until he decides to run his way out of his life crisis. As he runs the New York City Marathon to benefit AIDS research, he narrates how he defeated his fears and "the Other Shulman."

Zweibel is happy to admit that the novel is autobiographical. Overall, Zweibel is so happy that his e-mail address begins with "happyalan." (I kid you not.) He's had an amazing run as a writer—TV, plays, articles, jokes, screenplays, novels—not too long ago, Billy Crystal thanked him from the stage of the Tonys for helping him create "700 Sundays."

He grew up on Long Island, attended college in Buffalo and, at an early age, started selling jokes for $7 apiece to Borscht Belt regulars like Morty Gundy. After college, he took all the jokes that were too contemporary for those comics and started performing them at Manhattan clubs such as Catch a Rising Star and The Improv, where he first met Larry David and Crystal, who used to drive him in from Long Island.

One night after performing, he was approached by a young man who said, "You are the worst comedian I've ever seen." Zweibel agreed. But Lorne Michaels liked his writing and hired him for his new show, *Saturday Night Live.*

Zweibel's writing career has led to working with such diverse talents as Gilda Radner (their friendship inspired *Bunny, Bunny,* a successful book and stage play that mixed fact and fiction), Eddie Murphy, Garry Shandling (Zweibel co-created *It's Garry Shandling's Show*), Jesse Jackson (for his appearance hosting *Saturday Night Live*) and, more recently, Larry David on *Curb Your Enthusiasm.*

But a few years ago, Zweibel started to wonder about his life, his career and his marriage.

One day, he saw a flier offering to train people to run a marathon to benefit AIDS Project Los Angeles (APLA). Out of shape, and possibly out of his mind, he signed up. In 2001, he ran (and completed) the New York City Marathon, held just months after September 11. As he ran through the various New York City boroughs, Zweibel felt like he was running—and occasionally walking—through his life.

The plot for *The Other Shulman* arose out of that experience and a long-standing joke that goes: With all the weight he's lost over the years, there's another Zweibel out there. A portion of the book's proceeds are being donated to APLA.

Caveat emptor: If you are hankering for a challenging literary work set in the third world, look elsewhere. On the other hand, if you enjoy light summer reading that is comic, haimish and heartfelt, this is for you.

In another corner of the literary universe, Rosen's *Joy Comes in the Morning*, also deals with characters who are stuck, and also contains glimmers of autobiography.

Joy Comes in the Morning (a quote from Psalms) begins with the attempted suicide of one character and ends with the successful self-inflicted death of another. Between these two events, a science reporter, whose father is a Holocaust survivor succumbing to Alzheimer's, falls for a young female rabbi who is dealing with her own crisis of faith. It is a love story, but filled with the complications of two people searching for themselves even as they search for each other. A friend of mine, whom I shall refer to as "The Shrink," describes Rosen's novel approvingly as "the sexy woman rabbi book."

Picasso said, "Art is a lie that tells the truth." That is particularly true of Rosen's *Joy*. Rosen, the author of *Eve's Apple* and *The Talmud and the Internet*, is a friend who was my editor at The Forward. So I know how well he mined the personal raw data of his life—his wife is a rabbi, and his late father was a refugee from Germany—to create altogether fictional characters that read true.

Rosen has charted new territory by writing a serious Jewish American novel (as opposed to an American Jewish novel). This may seem mere semantics, but the difference is evident in what drives the characters. The protagonists in *Joy* are not engaged in a flight from their Jewish forebears, or in a rush to assimilate; nor are they thumbing their noses at an America that does or does not embrace them.

To the contrary, *Joy* concerns young secular Jews engaged in becoming more Jewish. I won't call it a "Red State" novel, but it is about values, presenting the voice of a generation becoming more traditional not only in politics, but in religion, as well.

In sum: Two novels, very different, but each makes us consider what matters in our lives, and how our inner journeys can transform us and our relationships with those we love.

August 18, 2005

A HUNGARIAN MIND

By this point in the summer, I know that my devoted Tommywood readers are all wondering the same thing—be they sitting by the pool at the Sociéte des Bains de Mer in Monte Carlo, on their yachts sailing off the coast of Turkey or schvitzing in their New York apartments or Los Angeles homes.

They all want to know: How is he going to come up with another column about Hungarians?

Frankly I was wondering the same, until I got the most wonderful e-mail. No, not the one about a "very important business proposition for you" from my Nigerian friend, but an invitation to a portrait exhibit of Hungarian Nobel laureates being held at the Scenic Drive Gallery in Monrovia.

Faster than you can say Yoy Istenem (Oh my God), I loaded up the family—wife, daughter, mother-in-law—and headed for the hills of Monrovia.

Hollywood-centric as I am, I initially thought Monrovia was where *Duck Soup* took place, but it turns out to be a small community not far from Pasadena.

The Scenic Drive Gallery is the home and studio of successful Hungarian-born artist Susan Dobay, who decided, in her words, "to give back" by turning part of her home into a gallery that hosts quarterly exhibits. (Go online to see the gallery and Dobay's work at home.earthlink.net/~sedobay/index.html).

We knew we were getting close when I spotted a small blonde woman with large teased hair, impeccably dressed, wearing glittering jewelry, looking completely out of place in the summer heat, ascending the driveway of a deceptively typical ranch home.

Inside we found quite a crowd. Dr. Odon Kiraly, the trade commissioner of the Hungarian Consulate for Los Angeles was there, as well as Ferenc Bosenbacher, the consul general in Los Angeles of the Hungarian Republic.

All around me were many Los Angeles-based Hungarians (or "Hunkies" as I am wont to call them) of the old or older variety. Surrounding them were Hungarian painter Attila Boros' portraits of Nobel Prize winners of Hungarian birth or descent.

Although Boros himself could not make the exhibit, his paintings each conveyed a great amount of personality. Boros' portraits combine photographic precision of their subjects' faces, while using the background to paint a subjective interpretation of each Nobel winner's genius.

So who are some of these Nobel Prize winners?

Elie Wiesel, who won the 1986 Peace Prize, was born in Sighet, Transylvania. Budapest-born Imre Kertesz, who won the 2002 Prize in literature, may be familiar to readers of this column for *Fateless*," his 1975 novel. Economist Milton Friedman, of the famous Chicago School of Economics, who was born in Brooklyn to Hungarian parents, is a 1976 winner.

John Haransyi, who as a Hungarian Jew spent part of World War II in a forced labor camp, may not be a household name, but he shared his 1994 mathematics Nobel with John Nash of "A

Beautiful Mind" fame. Eugene Wigner, the founder of nuclear engineering, responsible for the Manhattan Project idea was a 1962 winner (he also shared the Atoms for Peace award with fellow Hungarian Leo Szilard); Dennis Gabor, received a Nobel in 1971 for developing holography.

And there was my personal favorite, Albert Szent-Gyorgy. In my home, you see, when we talked about taking your Vitamin C, we didn't mention Linus Pauling. Instead we referenced Szent-Gyorgy, who received his prize for his pioneering work isolating Vitamin C.

And where did he find it?

As every Hungarian child knows, in paprika, of course.

This exhibit originated at the Koncz Gallery in Debrecen, Hungary. The gallery owner, Sandor Koncz, was present at the Monrovia event, and it's worth mentioning that the Koncz Gallery has, over the years, made it a mission to exhibit the art of Hungarian survivors of the Holocaust. The exhibition comes to Los Angeles from New York's Weinstein Gallery, which is operated by the Bnai Zion Foundation.

So, how is it that so many Hungarians, and so many Hungarian Jews, were able to express the mysteries of the universe in so many novel and Nobel ways?

My family members pondered this after the exhibition, during our salutary and gustatory stop in Pasadena at Pie 'n Burger (Pie 'n Burger is to In-N-Out as The Apple Pan is to Johnny Rockets—that is to say the authentic original, standing as an ideal, in the platonic shadow of a more successful chain of clones).

Perhaps to be a Hungarian Jew means to improvise—sometime to survive, sometimes to advance. And this ability—or necessity—to negotiate between culture and society, or between science and culture, has enabled these mainstream outsiders to climb towards and beyond the middle class. To innovate, to invent, to change the world.

Who knows? Perhaps they will one day discover some faulty gene that lies at the heart of this record of achievement. I wish I could figure it out—because the Hungarian who does will probably win a Nobel.

September 1, 2005

PRACTICE FOR SHAPIRO, MAKES PERFECT.

On Monday, September 19, at 9 p.m., the WB will premiere *Just Legal.* Produced by Jerry Bruckheimer, the current home-run king of TV, this is no *C.S.I.* clone, but rather a one-hour drama with occasional comic moments that is about the beauty, the promise, the reality and the heartbreak that is the American legal system.

Just Legal stars Don Johnson as Grant H. Cooper, a demoralized attorney who operates out of a Venice office, a block from the circus-like boardwalk, and for whom the Santa Monica Courthouse is home base. Cooper is so down and out that he no longer argues cases, he just settles or pleads them out. Jay Baruchel (from *Million Dollar Baby*) plays David "Skip" Ross, an idealistic young prodigy—emphasis on the young—he graduated college at fourteen, law school at seventeen and having passed the bar at eighteen, he's now trying to get a job. No one will hire him, other than Cooper whom he meets while caddying for him in a golf game in which Cooper successfully hustles his opponent. Cooper promises to get Ross into court fast—handling trials and showing him the way the real world really works. Will Cooper dash Ross' idealism? Will Ross manage to rekindle some of Cooper's former passion for the law? Of such questions is the pilot made.

Part of the show's appeal is the insights it offers into the law—as offered up by the show's creator, Jonathan Shapiro, an attorney turned television writer (*The Practice, Boston Legal*). Perhaps there is some irony in lawyers leaving the practice of law to write TV—about lawyers (ex-attorney and veteran TV producer Rob Bragin is also on the writing staff) but in some ways, Shapiro's intention is to portray both why people go into and why they consider leaving the law.

Like Shapiro, I, too, am a member of the NPLI (the non-practicing law institute), and perhaps that's why I find Shapiro's story—both his personal one, and the one he is trying to tell in *Just Legal*—so persuasive.

Born in Woodland Hills, Shapiro's father, Leonard, was a salesman for a furniture company and his mother, Deborah, was a bank teller—very hard-working people. They put their children's education ahead of their own advancement and their children did not disappoint.

Shapiro attended Harvard College (where he performed in Hasty Pudding shows) and was accepted to UC Berkeley's Boalt Law School. But he deferred admission to spend a year at Oxford University.

Did I mention that Shapiro was a Rhodes Scholar? And that his sport was boxing?

Holy Max Baer! While at Oxford, he saw that Frank Bruno had an upcoming bout in London. He couldn't afford a ticket so he contacted The Ring magazine and asked if he could be a stringer. Bruno knocked his contender out of the ring and Shapiro got his first paid writing gig.

Shapiro continued to write for The Ring. At the same time, he became a stringer for UPI. He decided he wanted to become a writer and told his father he was going to skip law school and go to work for a newspaper.

His father said: "I've never asked you to do anything. I ask you to go to law school." He also said the words that many Jewish fathers have told their children over the years, mine included: "Writing's not a real job. You've got to have a profession. You can always fall back on the law."

So he went to law school. Shapiro continued to write for *The Ring,* where he became its first-ever humor columnist, and for legal publications. At law school, Shapiro discovered a profound respect for the legal system: "The best part of democracy," Shapiro says, "happens in a courtroom."

Upon graduation, Shapiro became a federal prosecutor, working for the U.S. Justice Department, first in Washington, D.C., Superior Court and then as part of a Justice Department task force fighting organized crime, and then public corruption.

In Shapiro's office on the Sony lot, there's a framed letter from former U.S. Attorney General Janet Reno thanking him for helping prepare the Waco hearings.

Shapiro, by his own admission, "loved practicing law." His years as a prosecutor "defined me as a person."

He describes himself as unabashedly patriotic and as someone who very much enjoyed putting away the bad guys. Perhaps that part is genetic: As a bank teller, Shapiro's mother was held up at gunpoint four times, and always provided accurate IDs of the robbers, then went to work the next day.

Shapiro became involved in California government as chief of staff for Lt. Gov. Cruz Bustamente in the Gray Davis administration. When Bustamante lost his bid for governor, Shapiro found himself, at thirty-five, wondering what to do. He was, at the time, an adjunct professor of law at USC, and also worked occasionally as a judge pro-tem in Small Claims Court.

Shapiro decided that the time had come to try writing full time. His wife, successful comedy writer Betsy Borns (*All of Us, Roseanne, Friends*), encouraged him to write a sample TV script. (Betsy and I worked together at Interview Magazine in the Warhol era.) Shapiro wrote a spec *Practice* which got him a meeting with a producer on the show who asked him, "Did anything funny ever happen in court?" Shapiro related an anecdote about a judge who sentenced his charges based on their reaction to a very corny lecture he gave them. By the end of the meeting Shapiro had an assignment, and then a job on *The Practice,* which led to a being a producer on *Boston Legal.*

The inspiration for *Just Legal* was close to home. Despite Shapiro's impressive academic resume, turns out that in his family, he was always considered "the slow one." Shapiro had an older brother who was a prodigy, skipping grades, finishing law school at UCLA while still a teenager. However, upon graduation, his age worked against him—no major firm wanted to hire him. This is part of the inspiration for David "Skip" Ross.

At the same time, Shapiro based Don Johnson's character on three lawyers he knew "at the end of their careers."

"They were dump trucks," Shapiro says. "They never took anything to trial. They were like the [old] guys at boxing gyms."

Shapiro wanted to explore how they got that way. More than anything, he wanted to express "the idealism of the law versus the reality."

"The law is perfect," Shapiro said recently, "the problem is that [the practice of] of law is fundamentally heartbreaking."

My own experience and opinion of the law, overall, is quite similar to Shapiro's, if not as glamorous.

Although it would be easy to say that I only went to law school because of my parents—I was around three or four when my parents first told me I was going to be a lawyer—the truth is that I enjoyed law school. I found it intellectually challenging, I was surrounded by bright people, and I liked being in school.

The practice of law was another matter. I have discovered that in life, no matter what it is you do, after a few years you are in the business of doing it. That realization, and how you respond to it, determines your professional life, and to a great extent, the quality of your life.

Although I was at times gratified by doing right by my clients, I just did not find the practice of law satisfying. Granted, I was a single person in my twenties and many aspects of being an attorney that held no appeal then—a regular paycheck, being able to support a family, health care, support staff and the camaraderie of an office—all those I appreciate now and understand why my father desired them for me.

Moreover, there was a large gap between attorneys and the law as showcased in law school, and the ways in which the role of the attorney has evolved in recent years.

Once upon a time, lawyers were "counselors at law," trusted advisers. Young attorneys joined law firms with dreams of being made partner in seven or eight years, and then being set for life. The law firms themselves were institutions meant to outlive their founders and each represented a particular culture. They conferred prestige and status and were gateways into a way of living: partners had clubs they lunched at and country clubs they belonged to and there were charities and public institutions they participated in. To a great extent, they felt protected from the economic vagaries their clients faced.

If it seems as if I am talking about the era when Fitzgerald wrote Gatsby, the practice of law seemed like a throwback to that time, even in my day. Attorneys looked down on investment bankers—they were the people not smart enough to get into law school.

Then, in the late 1980s and 1990s as leveraged buyouts started to take hold, things changed. Status went to the dealmakers, and suddenly, the lawyers were simply the guys doing the paperwork, cleaning up after the bankers. Suddenly, the best, the brightest and the greediest were heading to work at investment banks. The practice of law seemed dull and old fashioned.

Suddenly, attorneys at law firms started looking at their own deals—name partners were pushed aside, not everyone became partner (nonequity partners), and lawyers increasingly split off to form new firms, concerned with their present earnings and with no real eye to institution building.

Today, the business of law has evolved. In California, lawyers, particularly in the entertainment sector, work on a commission basis—once upon a time, and certainly in New York, the very idea of having a stake in the financial outcome of a client's transaction would have appeared to be a conflict of interest. However, today, a lawyer receiving a percentage just means that he or she is even more your advocate.

One can argue that in California, lawyers, in general, and entertainment, new media and technology attorneys, in particular, have returned to being trusted advisers. These attorneys are not advising exclusively on legal matters as much as they are consigliere, partners in a career and a business. They have become part agent, part manager, part consultant, part strategic adviser without really having to have day-to-day responsibility for a business. At the same time, their own financial risk is spread out among their portfolio of clients. But, again, that speaks to the business of being a lawyer, and is something quite apart from the law itself.

For me, the farther I got away from the business of being a lawyer, the more I came to respect the legal system. The law gave me the opportunity to be a book author—and write about the Demjanjuk trial in Israel. Sitting in a courtroom for many long months gave me a great appreciation of the rule of law as the defining instrument of an open society.

To cite a few examples: Nelson Mandela, both a boxer and an attorney, is a great hero and a great role model, because he chose the rule of law to effect a peaceful revolution—even though he had been a victim of his country's apartheid system. In this country, similarly, we honor Martin Luther King, for his nonviolent protest by which he both defied and used the legal system to transform civil rights in our time.

In the pilot of *Just Legal,* Ross says, "Every great cause in this country was fought by trial lawyers; every great injustice was fixed by them."

Think about it.

In Israel, the Supreme Court has come to be regarded as the final arbiter of difficult social issues—and whether the world recognizes it or not, Israel's willingness to enforce its law against its own people in recent days—even dragging settlers out of synagogues, should go into the history books as a signal event in the history of democracy in the Middle East, a modern Altalena. A standard we can only hope to see exercised one day in Palestine and other Middle Eastern nations.

So, just as *The West Wing* sought to remind us that people who work in government are there for altruistic and not cynical reasons, Shapiro's *Just Legal* strives to remind us what the law can be.

"Half the show is about the idealism of how a young lawyer starts his career," Shapiro told me, "and the other half is about how an old lawyer recaptures his passion for the practice of law." And it is about how the system works: "The inequities of rich versus poor, the power of the state—all these play out in the courtroom."

Just Legal is also "about fathers and sons and about mentors who are the opposite of paternal figures."

And *Just Legal* is also about Cervantes' *Don Quixote.*

Shapiro acknowledged that while writing the pilot he was reading the wonderful new translation of *Don Q* by Edith Grossman (Harper & Collins) and here, and there, it seeped in. The close viewer will find references to the steed Rocinante and the fair Dulcinea. However, the roles of Don Quixote and Sancho Panza are not so obvious as it appears. Although it is young Ross who begins as caddy, he is the one on a quest and most likely to tilt at windmills. At the same time, anyone who judges Grant Cooper a fool, will find him as wily as the Man of la Mancha. Imagine *Don Q* on the WB!

Justice Oliver Wendell Holmes Jr., remarked: "The Life of the law has not been logic: it has been experience."

Based on the pilot, I can't say whether *Just Legal* will become a hit. But I can say, that based on its ambition, I'll be setting my Tivo on Season Pass and hoping it succeeds.

September 8, 2005

MISSING NEW ORLEANS

I've always kept a mental list of places about to disappear, such as the ruins of Angor Wat in Cambodia. Never—ever—was New Orleans on that list.

My first visit to New Orleans was as a college student, driving thirty-six hours straight from Vermont to attend Mardi Gras. I kept returning—with the annual Jazzfest becoming the ritual adult vacation for me, my wife and a gathering of friends.

On that first trip so many years ago, I climbed over the wall of the St. Louis No. 1 cemetery and played a game of tag with friends among the mausoleums and statuaries that still haunts me to this day. Even then, we didn't need Anne Rice to tell us New Orleans was a place that spoke about the epic struggle between life and death, where vampire and horror stories came to life, where voodoo and gris-gris made music. And the food was to die for.

New Orleans, with its gumbo-like history of French, Spanish and Arcadian influences, was a port city, and that meant Jews settled there and were part of its great history. You have but to walk downtown and see the names of old-time retailers such as the Rubinstein Brothers' store to get the idea.

And let's not forget that it was Morris Karnofsky, a Jewish peddler, who bought Louis Armstrong his first cornet, sharing with him a family feeling that Armstrong valued so greatly that he wore a necklace with a Jewish star for the rest of his life.

Occasionally you read about someone saying they saw Caruso sing, or Babe Ruth hit a homer. Well, I saw Professor Longhair play in New Orleans. I heard Dr. John and the Radiators at Tipitina's, Irma Thomas at the Lion's Den and Ellis Marsalis at Snug Harbor. I danced to Tribe Nunzio at Café Brasil, saw the Iguanas at the Mid-City Lanes Rock 'n' Bowl Nightclub and Marcia Ball at Jimmy's.

New Orleans was the Purim carnival to end all Purim carnivals.

One highlight of my life was a night at Preservation Hall, when the band invited me to join them on kazoo for an encore of "When the Saints Go Marching In." They gave me a solo.

Many are the memorable musical moments at Jazzfest, in the Gospel Tent, at Congo Square. But among them, one outshines the rest: standing in the rain to hear Randy Newman sing "Louisiana."

A Jewish angle? One night after hearing the New Orleans Klezmer All-Stars play at the Dragon's Den, a rumor spread that Adam Duritz (the lead singer of Counting Crows) was playing an unannounced set at a club on Toulouse Street. He came on at 2:30 a.m. and played till around 5. When I left, there were still people in the bars.

I don't mean to sentimentalize the city.

New Orleans may have been one of the poorest, most crime-ridden cities in America. Once after leaving Crabby Jack's on Highway 90, we witnessed a bank robbery in progress. I lost my appetite for a full fifteen minutes.

That city had to be one of the most obese in America. I can

understand why. One of the dishes I miss most was worth waiting in line at Jacques Imo's for: the deep-fried roast beef po'boy. You heard me: the New Orleans version of a roast beef hero, with all the fixings, dipped in batter and then deep-fried.

My idea of moderation was that for fifty-one weeks of the year we didn't live in New Orleans.

You are talking to a man who ate a dish called "debris" at Mother's, to someone who looked forward each visit to the Camellia Grill's chili-cheese omelet, with a pecan waffle on the side, a coffee milkshake and a dessert of pecan pie from the grill.

And nothing was better than ending up, or starting out, at Café du Monde for beignets and chicorée café au lait.

New Orleans was unhealthy in oh-so-many ways but that doesn't mean it wasn't the happiest city in America. I smiled from the moment I landed and kept smiling for weeks after I left.

The smiles will be a long time returning. Our friends, the Suttons, owned several jewelry stores downtown and will now relocate. I haven't heard yet what happened to Al Palma, our Argentine-Jewish cab driver who became part of our regular crew. Al always said of New Orleans: "You got to know people here, and you don't know people."

But we did: We knew Al, for one, and I hope he's OK.

New Orleans will rebuild. It is inevitable. People still live on the hillsides below Mt. St. Helens and Pompeii. After World War II, they rebuilt London and Warsaw and Berlin. People returned to downtown Manhattan after September 11 and we continue to live in California along the fault lines.

Man is stupid—and loyal. If history has taught us anything it is that we have an enormous capacity to forget tragedy and to ignore its lessons. That's part of what makes us human. And New Orleans is all about being human—in the best and worst ways.

The city may never be the same. But then again, what is and who is? New Orleans'll be back one day and I'll be there, too, at the first chance. Missing the New Orleans that was. Enjoying the New Orleans that will be.

September 22, 2005

WIESENTHAL THE COLLECTOR

Simon Wiesenthal died last month at ninety-six in his sleep at his home in Vienna. This seems particularly fitting, since Wiesenthal spent the last sixty years troubling the sleep of Nazi war criminals, their henchmen, collaborators and supporters.

During the Holocaust, eighty-nine members of Wiesenthal's extended family were murdered, including his mother who was deported to the Belzec extermination camp. Wiesenthal himself was a prisoner at a succession of charnel houses, such as the Janovska camp, Plaszow (the camp in "Schindler's List"), Auschwitz, Buchenwald and Mauthausen, where the Americans liberated him in May 1945.

Wiesenthal soon compiled a list of every Nazi persecutor he had come across during the war and began collecting evidence for the War Crimes Section of the U.S. Army.

As Jewish refugees and concentration camp survivors flooded Austria's displaced persons camps from Eastern Europe, Wiesenthal saw a unique opportunity to gather testimony of war crimes. At the same time, the criminals, the Nazis, were still on the loose, many still in Austria and Germany. In 1947, Wiesenthal set up an office in Linz, Austria, and began his life's work, which he continued until a few years ago.

My late father, Bruce Teicholz, and Wiesenthal were friends. They were contemporaries, both born in Galicia, that part of the Austro-Hungarian Empire that is now Ukraine. Before the war, both had lived and worked in Lvov (known today as Lviv); both remained there during the 1939 Soviet occupation, and each escaped after the Nazis arrived in 1941 (although Wiesenthal was apprehended).

After the war, they found each other in Austria. Whether they had known each other in Lvov or met in Vienna, I can't say, but they were bonded by their shared background. At the time, my father was the designated representative of the former concentration camp inmates and Jewish displaced persons (DPs) in Austria, and as such, had dealings with the four occupying powers, as well as with the Jewish Agency and the Bricha, the precursor to the Haganah. Wiesenthal often came from Linz to meet with my father, seeking support for his work.

In later years, they stayed in touch. They sent each other Jewish New Year cards, and I recall Wiesenthal as a guest in our home in New York on more than one occasion. I remember him because we shared a mutual interest in stamp collecting (more on that later).

Although now remembered as "the conscience of the Holocaust," over the years, Wiesenthal was accused by some of being an egomaniac, an opportunist, a man who lived off the Holocaust, a liar who exaggerated his own accomplishments, a bungler who reported false sightings of Mengele and then refused to believe he was dead (when he was).

And although he was most often described as a "Nazi hunter," during his dispute with Austrian Chancellor Bruno Kreisky,

Kreisky implied that Wiesenthal had been a Nazi collaborator—never offering any evidence to support his claim. And some labeled Wiesenthal an apologist for U.N. Secretary General and Austrian President Kurt Waldheim, when Waldheim's Nazi past came to light.

My father knew Wiesenthal well enough not to excuse his occasional failings but to set them in context. Wiesenthal's personality, with its several foibles, was also the basis for his lasting legacy and well-deserved renown.

It's important to understand that two developments had a serious impact on Wiesenthal's early post-war work. First, by the late 1940s, the Nuremberg trials were, for all intents and purposes over. As Abby Mann dramatized so effectively in *Judgment at Nuremberg,*" the growing Cold War created pressure to end the war crimes trials and enlist Germany as an ally against the Soviet Union.

Also by 1953, the displaced persons administration in Austria was dismantled. Its work, too, was deemed over. The DPs had all gone to start new lives, many in the U.S. and Israel. Without witnesses and without trials, Wiesenthal's work seemed at an end.

In 1954, he formally closed his Documentation Center office in Linz, and transferred his files to the Holocaust archives at Yad Vashem in Israel. Wiesenthal himself remained in Austria, moving to Vienna. He continued to work with refugees from Eastern Europe, organizing language and rehabilitation courses.

Then in 1960, Israeli agents captured Adolf Eichmann in Buenos Aires and brought him to stand trial in Jerusalem. The publicity convinced Wiesenthal to return to Nazi hunting. He opened a small office in Vienna.

Wiesenthal's decision was not met with universal approval and support. At the time, Nazi hunting was not on anyone's list of accepted private professions—and although Wiesenthal lived modestly—some thought it unseemly when he requested funds to support himself and his work in Vienna of all places.

Holocaust survivors were, for the most part, focused on building new lives in new countries. Israel was offered up as the answer to the Holocaust. To many, the right place to archive Nazi documentation was in Israel, with its large population of survivor witnesses. Tuviah Friedman, a colleague of Wiesenthal's in Austria, opened the Haifa Documentation Center. The Israel police created a Nazi-hunting unit.

Further, Wiesenthal's decision to make a full-time career of Nazi hunting seemed odd. Holocaust remembrance was something to be done, if at all, in one's spare time, like charity work. What could one private citizen do—as opposed to a government prosecutor, or an academic, or even a journalist?

Despite all this, Wiesenthal set about his work.

Did Wiesenthal have an ego? Of course. How else could one man think that what he did, alone in an office, without government aid, mattered and persuade others of that as well?

Over the years, Wiesenthal was publicly at odds with prominent figures, such as Elie Wiesel, Mossad Chief Isser Harel, Serge and Beate Klarsfeld, Edgar Bronfman and Eli Rosenbaum. All I can say is that perhaps there was a reason Wiesenthal was best suited to working alone.

Wiesenthal was said to have aided in the capture of more than 1,100 Nazis. Although this may not be not strictly true, to call it untrue is to misunderstand what Wiesenthal accomplished.

Wiesenthal did not personally capture Eichmann. Nor did he provide Israel with the specific tip that led to Eichmann, who lived under the name Ricardo Klement in Buenos Aires.

As the Simon Wiesenthal Center, to its credit, states in its official bio of Wiesenthal, in 1954 he supplied information to the Israeli Embassy in Vienna that Eichmann was in Argentina. It was only in 1959, when Israeli intelligence received information from Fritz Bauer, a West German prosecutor, that they sent agents to Buenos Aires to abduct Eichmann.

Yet it was Wiesenthal who insisted that Eichmann not be declared dead, as his widow requested as early as 1947. Wiesenthal kept the hunt for Eichmann alive, literally, until Eichmann was apprehended, and for that he deserves praise.

Information Wiesenthal gathered led to many significant prosecutions. There was the arrest of Karl Silberbauer, the Gestapo aide who arrested Anne Frank—at a time when Holocaust deniers questioned the veracity of her published diary.

He also found Majdanek camp guard Hermine Braunsteiner-Ryan, who was living as a Queens housewife. The notion that this seemingly retiring person had been a notoriously sadistic tormentor did as much, if not more, to wake up people to the everyday quality of participants in the Final Solution as did seeing Eichmann in a glass booth.

In Brazil, Wiesenthal located Franz Stangl, the Treblinka commandant, responsible for the deaths of more than 870,000 Jewish men, women and children in little more than a year. He was extradited to stand trial in Germany. Also in the 1980s, Wiesenthal was able to locate and bring pressure to bear on extraditing and prosecuting SS officer Josef Schwammberger.

This latter case touched some close family friends, the Tuchmans, who lived in the same building as my family on

West End Avenue in New York. I went to high school with Jeff Tuchman. His father, Dr. Marcel Tuchman, still remembers Schwammberger and the way he used his German shepherd dog, Prince, to sadistically prey on Jewish inmates.

Dr. Tuchman flew to Germany to give testimony at Schwammberger's trial. Being able to do so was, as the credit card commercials say, priceless.

Stangl died in jail in 1971; Schwammberger died in prison in 2004. At each step of their final journey, there were press accounts detailing their evil deeds. Wiesenthal outlived them both. There was justice in that, a little vengeance and some measure of satisfaction.

Over the years Wiesenthal wrote books, consulted on movies and even had Ben Kingsley portray him on the screen in the HBO movie, *Murderers Among Us*. This, too, is his legacy.

Wiesenthal and his work have been irresistible subjects for books and films. As I write this, Tony Stern, another high school friend, has the rights to Wiesenthal's *The Sunflower* and is developing adaptations for the screen and the stage, as well as planning a documentary film.

Wiesenthal relished the awards he received from all over the world, including an honorary knighthood from the queen of England. He was disappointed not to win the Nobel (and miffed that Wiesel received it alone in 1986).

But it was Wiesenthal who became an international "brand" in 1977 by making what amounted to a licensing deal with the founders of the Simon Wiesenthal Center, an organization dedicated to the ideals of combating anti-Semitism and promoting tolerance (a somewhat more abstract elucidation of Wiesenthal's own specific quest to document and prosecute the crimes of the Holocaust in the name of the victims). The organization's success and popularity insures Wiesenthal a degree of immortality.

In the end, Wiesenthal's accomplishments are larger and deeper than mere words such as "justice" or "vengeance." Wiesenthal labored to ensure that what occurred was not forgotten.

As for those who committed the crimes and believed that doing so was permissible—or that no one would ever know, or ever care, or that there would be no consequence, no shame for doing so—they were all wrong.

A side note: Wiesenthal trained to be an architect, and was certified as an architectural engineer. The obits say he never practiced after the war, but I do recall seeing among the papers my father donated to the YIVO Institute for Jewish Research a Wiesenthal drawing for a proposed Holocaust memorial.

There was indeed architecture to his mission. He essentially created a structural foundation for Nazi war crimes prosecution. He collected evidence; he researched. And as part of his repertoire of tactics, he held press conferences and he badgered—when others cared little or, certainly, cared less.

Perhaps the best way to think of Wiesenthal is as a collector. Collecting stamps was his beloved hobby. And in much the same way, he collected criminals.

At the end of the war, he drew up his list. Over the years, he refined and added to that list. Like many a stamp collector, he was happiest alone with his papers in his office, working at his collection, and happier still when he was able to sequester a hard-to-find Nazi criminal and close the book on him.

October 6, 2005

WHO'S YOUR MUMMY?

On a day when a hot desert wind whipped through town, I found myself in a darkened chamber contemplating death and the afterlife—not my own, for a change, but rather that of the ancient Egyptians.

Currently the LA area is hosting two world-class exhibitions of ancient Egyptian artifacts: King Tut has taken up residence in Mid-Wilshire in the LACMA annex. Less than an hour away, in Santa Ana (of the eponymous hot winds), the Bowers Museum is showcasing one of the greatest exhibits of mummies ever seen in the United States from the collection of the British Museum.

Together, the two exhibitions offer more Egyptian artifacts and mummies on view in America than at any time since Boris Karloff played Im-ho-Tep. Since Howard Carter first uncovered Tutankhamun's tomb in 1922, we have always known more about how ancient Egyptians died than how they lived. Our fascination has manifested itself in comedy and horror, scholarship and satire: from Abbott & Costello to the recent Brendan Fraser resurrections; from the Saturday morning cartoon "Tutenstein" to the record-breaking ticket sales for past and current Tut exhibitions.

Tutankhamun and the Golden Age of the Pharoahs displays fifty Tut burial objects, including the gold crown found on his mummified body and more than seventy items from his family and other members of the Eighteenth Dynasty, who reigned around 3,500 years ago. Displayed over almost a dozen galleries, each is focused on a specific theme, such as "daily life in Tutankhamun's world," "the tomb" and of course, "the gift shop."

It is hard not to be impressed by the artistry, the sophistication and the sheer beauty of the jewelry and crafts. The collection includes stunning necklaces, chalices, statues and even ornately carved wooden seats.

The exhibit also discusses some of the more interesting aspects of King Tut's reign. Tut, who assumed the throne as child of nine or ten and died no more than a decade later, was known for reintroducing polytheism to Egypt. His predecessor, Akhenopten, had decided to abolish all gods other than the Sun disk and also to move the capital city. Tut's restoration of the prior capital and the gods proved popular in his time.

Was it his decision or that of a close adviser? No one knows.

I see the movie now: Imagine a mysterious figure, who haunts political figures, giving them spin on how to cast a spell over the public—Tut refers to him as his "architect"; others call him "Tut's brain." After the tomb of Tut is disturbed for the 1979 American tour, he escapes in Texas and makes his way to Crawford under the name Karl Rove. Now, that's spooky!

For the *C.S.I.* generation, the final gallery is devoted to CT scans made recently of Tut's corpse, which suggest that he may have died from infection following a fracture in his leg.

Tut himself didn't make this trip to LACMA. So if it's actual mummies you want, head down to Santa Ana. The Bowers Museum exhibit is a world-class lesson in mummification and the Egyptian cult of the dead: There are fourteen mummies and/or coffins on view. Artifacts include a mummy mask, a child's coffin and many accoutrements of Egyptian-style death, including canoptic jars in which the organs were preserved and a small wooden boat meant to transport the dead into the underworld (warning: funeral objects appear larger in the afterlife). Also one was expected to work in the afterlife, but you could have shebtis, or little servants, to help you. Apparently, good help is easy to find in the afterlife.

Mary Roach's new book, *Spook* (Norton), tries to find scientific support for an afterlife. Her book reminds us that throughout history, man has searched for proof of an afterlife, from Herophilus, to DaVinci, to ectoplasm and spirit mediums in the 1920s. Many believed their afterlife to be more important than their corporeal, scientifically verifiable one.

Personally, I side with an Egyptian, but not a member of the Tut clan. This one lived in the twelfth century and is best known as "the Rambam." I speak of the Jewish philosopher Maimonides, who argued that we are best served by considering the afterlife as true, but also as allegorical and metaphorical. Author Sherwin Nuland's forthcoming biography, called, *Maimonides* (Shocken/Nextbook), explains this in greater detail.

I believe in past lives—in a Rambam way: I feel with all my soul that I once was a slave in Egypt. As I make way around present day Los Angeles, I carry with me the voices of the people who have come before me. They are my forebears, both literally and spiritually, and they are always present in my thoughts, conversations and my actions.

The people who have an afterlife are those we remember by day and by night in our dreams and in our prayers—family members as much as poets, authors, singers and songwriters, biblical, historical and literary figures, fading in and out of popularity within the collective consciousness of any age.

As for King Tut, he lived only nineteen years, and yet thousands of years later, he is still among us, still on tour, because grave robbers couldn't find his tomb before Carter did. Is this kind of immortality a reward or a curse? I say it's one more mystery of the afterlife for us to ponder.

October 20, 2005

IN SEARCH OF...HIMSELF

The High Holidays are always a good time to reflect, and this year, as I was serially sermonized in ways both inspirational and depressing, I was asked to consider that we can always start anew—that, as the dorm posters used to say, "Today is the first day of the rest of your life."

Which reminds me of what Reb Jackie Mason said on the subject: "If we live every day like it's the last day of our lives ... one day we'll be right."

So as we play the TiVo of our lives, do we fixate on certain events, moments, relationships, and wonder what might have been? Or do we—can we—move on?

Which brings me to *When It Comes to Women,* Bruce Goldsmith's new play currently playing at the Odyssey Theater in Los Angeles.

Despite its title, Goldsmith's play is not a *Jake's Women* review of the women in his life—rather it is a funny, at times sad and poignant, exploration of a "hinge" moment in one person's life—how it impacts and reverberates on his relationships. It is about how loyalties and betrayals play out among fathers and sons, mothers and sons, husbands and wives.

When It Comes to Women asks what seem like impossible questions: What would happen if only I could talk honestly and openly with my parents about the true challenges in their marriage and in my own relationships, and about our own real feelings of self-worth? Could they respond with equal honesty? Can we ever find the love from our father and from our mother that we are searching for? Can we ever recapture the joy of a first love? What are the compromises we are willing to make in our marriages? Is it all a matter of the road not taken?

In Goldsmith's play, we see—in a way the lead character cannot—the impact of the stubbornness and of the lack of kindness, charity, compassion and connection that can and does occur in one's life. We see the wreckage incurred, the human cost of a damaged soul. We are witness to, Goldsmith says, a man's search "to find some sense of himself, to overcome confusion."

Goldsmith, with whom I served on the board of PEN USA, the writers' human rights organization, is given to humor and seriousness in equal measure. His play, he says, is about "death and smoked fish." Goldsmith asks: "What could be more Jewish than that?"

The playwright's own story has had its twists and turns. His grandparents on both sides were Russian Jewish immigrants who led, as he put it, "heroic lives" to come to this country. Although born in Chicago, Goldsmith was raised in Los Angeles. He graduated from USC film school, where he won praise as a director.

To better understand the process of acting, he joined the Actors and Directors Lab, studying under such luminaries as Jack Garfein, Harold Clurman and William Inge and such incendiaries as Henry Miller. He spent four years there and fell in love with the process of creating drama in a scene.

It was as a screenwriter, however, that Goldsmith found gainful employment, writing feature scripts for Fox, Warner

Bros. and Paramount, among others. Over time, he found himself most drawn to the small, yet critical, moments in people's lives, which he judged better suited for the page than the market-driven large screen. He decided to write a novel.

In 1986, *Strange Ailments; Uncertain Cures,* Goldsmith's first novel, "literally changed my life," he now says. Not only did he sell the movie rights, but he wrote the screenplay adaptation and suddenly found himself in demand as a screenwriter. *Strange Ailments* has been continually optioned ever since. Goldsmith believes that it will get made. When? "Soon."

Goldsmith followed *Strange Ailments* with *Blue Numbers* (Mercury House) and *The Hard R Marathon* (Burning Gate Press). Still, he yearned to return to the stage. There is, Goldsmith says, "something about the intimacy" of it happening in front of you. He continues to be fascinated by the "struggle of what makes a scene work."

The plot of *When It Comes to Women* takes place from 1971 to 1994, as a young man goes from idealistic single, to married father; from entrepreneurial dreams to business success (as an importer of gourmet foods and smoked fish). Goldsmith's solution to creating a "narrative drive" over a twenty-three year period was to focus on a series of critical moments, and let the audience fill in the rest. Goldsmith discovered that "moments have a cumulative power," both intense and involving.

A talented cast features David Shatraw in the lead role, supported by veterans Millie Slavin and F. William Parker (playing his parents). Jenny Eakes and Christina Haag portray the women in his life. The ensemble conveys the passage of time not with makeup but through the power of acting.

Goldsmith and I had lunch the Monday after his play opened. In reviewing his writing career, he concluded: "You have to pursue things that you find immensely important and write them."

To sit and watch Goldsmith's play is to ask: Are we the prisoners of the events in our lives? Is there free will? Can we break our patterns? Can we change? Can we move on? Who is there to help us? Or are we essentially alone?

This, in sum, is what Goldsmith's play is about—only it's funnier and more entertaining than the seriousness those topics would imply.

And as I said to Goldsmith at lunch, "What's more important than that?"

November 3, 2005

THE POWER OF THE PAINTED BIRD

Forty years ago this October. 15, Houghton Mifflin published *The Painted Bird* by Jerzy Kosinski. The book was immediately acclaimed as a must-read text on the Holocaust and the nature of human cruelty.

In the years leading up to and following Kosinski's 1991 suicide, his reputation was tarnished by a series of revelations that the author employed uncredited editors and associates to produce his novels, and that much of Kosinski's personal history was fabricated.

Nonetheless, the reputation of *The Painted Bird* has endured. Grove, which has published *The Painted Bird* in paperback since 1995, won't divulge sales figures, but a sales rep called it "one of the mainstays of our backlist."

I reread the 1965 original first edition, as well as the edition currently on the shelves, which Kosinski revised and published with a new introduction in 1976. (There are notable differences between the two.) I wanted to understand the novel's continued appeal.

The Painted Bird is the story of a young boy, age six when the novel begins, whose parents, to protect him, consign him to a family in the country at the start of World War II. When his caretaker dies, he wanders from village to village until the war's end, witnessing and suffering acts of cruelty and perversion. After one particular incident, he becomes mute.

After liberation, he falls under the spell of a few Red Army soldiers, who leave him at an orphanage until his parents reclaim him. At age sixteen, after a skiing accident, he regains his speech.

The novel spends almost the first hundred pages without even mentioning the Nazis, detailing instead the lives and folk beliefs of rural peasants. Actually, the word Nazis is never used, only "the Germans."

A short section, about halfway through the book, describes the trains to the extermination camps—and they are cited toward the end of the book, as well. But for the most part, on its surface, the book has little to do with the Holocaust.

This is all the more interesting, given that we now know that *The Painted Bird* is not inspired by literal events in Kosinski's life, as some originally assumed. Kosinski spent the war years in relative safety, living with his parents under false papers.

In relation to both the Holocaust and the author's own life, *The Painted Bird* presents a series of metaphors and allegories through its vignettes of cruelty, perversion and humiliation—all tinged with sadism—more often than not culminating in rape.

The book's title refers to a tale of a bird whose feathers are painted, and because it is different, other birds attack it and kill it.

Some scenes are repulsive—I had recalled the episodes, but I had not remembered them as being so detached and gratuitous. More than once I put the book down, wondering why more readers were not offended by the book's contents, particularly at the time it was originally published.

Yet once I had finished the novel, I felt differently. I understood why the novel succeeds and remains popular to this day.

In part because *The Painted Bird* does not describe the Holocaust as we have come to know it, or any world as we know it, the reader implicitly accepts that the novel operates metaphorically.

Adolescents relate to this tale, in particular, because they are themselves in a state of war, a time of us vs. them, a time when youths feel most acutely that they are "different." It's a time when they feel besieged, tormented by peers and estranged from the adults surrounding them.

Adolescence is a time when children are beginning to separate from their parents; this separation occurs literally within the book.

Moreover, children in adolescence stand on the threshold of sex. Their notions and ideas and their introduction to what sex is, to how sexual relations are conducted, all are informed by the yearnings of hormonal surges.

For many children, their first glimpses of sexual acts—whether it be of animals or from pornographic or erotic materials—can convey a graphic vision of sex that is seemingly detached, demeaning, abusive or even violent. And yet, these images remain powerful and stimulating nonetheless. Again, this captivating repulsion is consistent with the scenes in "The Painted Bird," which present a heightened, more shocking version of reality, but one that resonates.

In the novel, Kosinski explains the murderous and deviant impulses of his characters within the context of the powerless and the powerful. At some level, Kosinski, who had a life-long fascination with S & M, presents the homicidal urge as an exercise of feeling power over another person.

At a remove of more than sixty years, the images we have of the Holocaust in Poland, of the ghettos and the camps, have an expected quality to them. Yet, *The Painted Bird* continues to offend, to disgust—and its haunting tales have an unexpected quality—in part because they remain unfamiliar to us. At the same time, these stories derive an added dimension, added power if you will, from being set during the war years and the period immediately following the war.

The novel's artistry is such that its ugliness rises to the level of importance. After reading the novel, one is prepared to accept, in a way one resists while reading it, that Kosinski's novel has served a purpose—that in an abstract way, it has explained something of the cruelty that caused humans to participate in the Holocaust, some with glee, some as a matter-of-everyday existence.

In this way, *The Painted Bird* rightly assumes its place as a work about the Holocaust—despite some troubling aspects. In one scene, a Jewish girl escapes from a train bound for the death camps, only to be raped to death. Kosinski seems to assert that it is better to die raped as a woman than incinerated as a Jew.

Beyond that, *The Painted Bird* argues that brutality against those who are different is part of nature—like the fate of the painted bird—and that the Holocaust was, sadly, not so unnatural. It was an all-too-possible aspect of human nature above and beyond the part played by the philosophy of National Socialism or by racism or by a Final Solution. Acceptance of the Holocaust, and participation in it, was part and parcel of the natural inclination of the peasantry who abhorred people different from themselves and often acted perversely and cruelly even among their own.

To universalize his message, Kosinski obscures specificity. Kosinski implies the boy is Jewish but never says so, hiding behind the possibility that he is Jewish or Gypsy or might just look Jewish or like a Gypsy.

Significantly, Kosinski changed the location of where the boy was wandering from Poland in the first edition to *Central Europe* in subsequent editions. Also during the war years, the two people who show mercy to the boy and let him escape are German soldiers—leaving us to wonder whether the peasants are not worse than even the Nazis.

Similarly, although the boy falls under the spell of Red Army soldiers, life under communist rule seems no less cruel than under the Germans. The boy takes to wandering his home city at night and exacts revenge on a boy by dropping a brick on his head.

In the revised edition, the novel ends with the boy regaining his speech. However, the original first edition concludes with a postscript that describes life under the communists as a place where the inner life is imprisoned as much as outer life was restricted under the Germans.

Kosinski's attempt to take a universal or sociological perspective to his narrative creates moments of moral relativism that belie the uniqueness of what the Nazis perpetrated against the Jews and the Gypsies and diminishes the role of their collaborators.

Today, the novel comes with a preface, called an "Afterword," written for the 1976 edition. In it, Kosinski explained that he wanted to write something that was separate from an autobiography.

For one thing, he intended the novel as a blow against the communist establishment. And it was received as such—Kosinski and his work were banned and attacked behind the Iron Curtain. He also pointed out that what happened in *The Painted Bird* was credible and sometimes less violent, horrible and cruel than what happened in the Holocaust itself.

In effect, Kosinski wanted it all: If it didn't happen to him, it was true nonetheless, and he was heroic in writing it, as he suffered and was attacked for having done so.

Given Kosinski's actual biography, this makes some sense. He wanted to write about what he knew—which was not the details of the Holocaust but a more detached experience within wartime Poland; he saw himself as both hero and victim of his own narrative.

As James Park Sloan details in his thorough 1996 biography of the author, Kosinski was born into an intellectual, assimilated Jewish family in Lodz, Poland. Although his extended family lost more than sixty members in the Holocaust, Kosinski did not personally witness atrocities.

During the war, he learned that lying was survival and that standing out could mean death. After the war, he grew up in a communist society devoid of religious practice or identity, where the state's interests outweighed those of the individual.

Kosinski came to the United States in 1957 as a sociology graduate student, and within a few years, he was writing nonfiction, explaining the Soviet collective mind to Western audiences.

It is not surprising that when Kosinski sat down to write fiction in the early 1960s, he chose to write about what he knew best. As he could not write about the Holocaust itself, Kosinski confabulated childhood and war.

Taught as a child to lie about his life, he did so again, ironically, in a work of fiction. He wrote about the dangers of being a painted bird—while playing the part himself by writing a novel in America about torture, sodomy and rape. Having been powerless, he became the master of his own destiny, playing out his fascination with sadism and with power. The resulting novel, *The Painted Bird* continues to fascinate, shock, disgust and compel us transcendently to this day.

November 24, 2005

THE GREAT QUESTION

We're almost halfway through the first decade of the twenty-first century. Not a bad time to assess *Who We Are.*

Who We Are: On Being (and Not Being) a Jewish American Writer, edited by Derek Rubin (Schocken Books, 2005), an Israeli-born professor who teaches in the Netherlands, collects 29 essays by Jewish American writers, some of which were previously published, others reshaped or written for this collection. The contributors span a chronological range from Saul Bellow, born in 1915, to Yael Goldstein, born in 1978, and include such familiar names as Philip Roth, E.L. Doctorow, Grace Paley, Chaim Potok, Alan Lelchuk, Erica Jong, Art Spiegelman, Nessa Rapoport, Robert Cohen, Jonathan Rosen and Allegra Goodman.

Some tell the stories of how they became Jewish writers or found their Jewish voice, others argue for a world of literature independent of ethnic distinctions. Still others argue for an even more Jewish literature, one inspired by and filled with references to Jewish liturgy, history and practice.

Who We Are is also a story of personal struggle, of how each contributor confronts the questions: Who am I?; what story do I have to tell?; and who am I writing for?

This collection comes at an interesting time in American Jewish letters, a time of great pluralism and creativity. At the risk of rehashing some of what I wrote in a longer essay about Jewish self-image in America for the USC Casden Institute's annual survey of the Jewish role in American life (vol. 1, USC, 2002), several points are worth repeating:

First of all: Who is a Jewish writer? Isaac Bashevis Singer once made a distinction between writers born Jewish and writers who "write Jewish" (he identified himself as the latter). By contrast, Norman Mailer, although born Jewish and a major American novelist, is rarely considered a "Jewish writer." Nor for that matter is David Leavitt, who finds himself more often in anthologies of gay literature. Nor is Michael Chabon, whose novels are often filled with Jewish references. But is this solely a matter of content?

Consider that many novels written by non-Jewish writers are filled with Jewish protagonists, such as John Updike's Bech novels. And non-Jewish writers have written important Holocaust-themed works, among them William Styron's "Sophie's Choice," and Thomas Keneally's *Schindler's List.*

So, if it's not purely a matter of the author's Jewishness or a novel's Jewish content, what then is American Jewish Fiction anyhow? The category was coined in the 1950s and early 1960s as a way to denote a generation of children or grandchildren of immigrants (Saul Bellow, Philip Roth, Bernard Melamud) raised in America and college educated, who took to the pages to riff on the yearning to be American—from their vantage point as outsiders. Their literary success was in its own way part of the American dream: The literary world was a far better, more refined place than the Jewish neighborhoods of Chicago and Newark where Bellow and Roth grew up.

The talent and energy in these writers' novels so energized American fiction that they provoked a thousand others to pen their own works, Jewish and non-Jewish, American and foreign—some inspired, some angered by what they had written.

American Jewish fiction found many different voices: the sacred and the profane in the work of Cynthia Ozick and Erica Jong; the magical and historic in that of Max Apple and Doctorow; the political and philosophical in Grace Paley and Rebecca Goldstein. More often than not, their fiction was characterized by a desire, like Joseph and the Pharoah, to interpret the dreams of the country they lived in.

By the end of the 1980s, however, it was generally acknowledged that the original troika of Bellow, Roth and Melamud had been so successful as to become completely assimilated into the academy and the establishment. Critics began to sound the death knell of American Jewish fiction as a distinctive genre. The romance of writing the great-American novel had lost its appeal as well as its position of importance in the culture. Talented young writers were applying to business school or getting jobs at Internet start-ups. They were writing business plans, not short stories. And if the creative voice inside them spoke, it told them to write screenplays.

However, despite dire predictions of its demise, American Jewish fiction is again flourishing in the 21st century. As Morris Dickstein remarked in a 1997 essay in Tikkun: "The current resurgence of Jewish-American writing in a world rife with assimilation is as surprising as the survival of the Jews themselves."

So what happened?

Permit me to chart this bumpy road with a quick survey of my own attitude toward this genre.

In high school, I wasn't much interested in "Jewish American fiction" or Bellow, Melamud and Roth. Joan Didion and Thomas Pynchon were the contemporary authors that I and my friends and teachers admired in school—and outside of class, there was Jack Kerouac, Richard Farina and Ken Kesey to lead us into the American underground.

I resisted Roth et al, because—how do I put it? In a word, I was, in my fashion, an anti-Semite.

Although I had never read any of these famous American Jewish authors, I had already judged them as "not interesting"—they wrote about a species that I called the "New American Jew"—today we might call them the Jewish American Prince and Jewish American Princess. I could not relate to these confections—they seemed inauthentic—neither American nor Jewish. The prince, I imagined to be a deracinated ubermensch, assimilated into nothing; the princess a creature too fantastical to be believed. In truth had I read the books then, I would have found a more complex portrayal of American Jews, but just a glimpse of Richard Benjamin and Paula Prentiss in the movie version of *Goodbye Columbus* put me off reading Roth for another decade.

I had no idea of what Jewish fiction should be, or even if it should be. Hemingway (with his fondness for the word "kike") and Fitzgerald (also not above the occasional slur, despite occasional bouts of semitophilia) were my idea of American fiction writers. To the extent that an American author of Jewish birth could match their achievements, fine.

But as the Bobster said, "I was so much older then."

Then a funny thing happened to me at Andy Warhol's Factory (not the original factory but the Union Square incarnation).

Gael Love, my editor at Interview magazine, appointed me her court Jew—and I mean that in the nicest possible way. Whenever there was an aged child of Abraham to interview she assigned him to me (Jerzy Kosinski, Isaac Bashevis Singer, Baron Guy de Rothschild, rock impresario Bill Graham). In order to keep up with my subjects, I began to read Jewish fiction.

I put aside my preconceptions and prejudices and experienced the exhilaration of reading *Augie March,* the splendor of Bellow's achievement standing as it does as a bridge between the nineteenth century novel with its echoes of Dickens and the twentieth century, speaking in a voice and language completely American yet completely his own. In Roth, I found an heir to Franz Kafka, Isaak Babel, Nikolai Gogol and Lenny Bruce. I reveled in the humor, wit and prodigious talent manifest in his novels, continuing to this day, a run without parallel in American literature.

But more remarkable than Roth and Bellow—who, let's face it, are remarkable by any standard in any category—are all their contemporaries and all the American Jewish writers who have followed them. Jerzy Kosinski, Cynthia Ozick, Singer, to name but a few whose books have given me many pleasurable hours.

As the 1980s came to an end—a period Tom Wolfe coined "The Me Decade," American Jewish writers found themselves secure in their identity as Americans with little personal experience of classical anti-Semitism. Whether learned or ignorant of Jewish texts and ritual, myriad new Jewish voices were unleashed, as diverse and colorful as Joseph's coat: female (Anita Diamant, Nomi Eve, Myla Goldberg), gay (Lev Raphael, Arye Lev Stollman), the formerly observant and the newly Orthodox (Pearl Abraham, Tova Mirvis, Dara Horn), the child survivor and the children of survivors (Louis Begley, Thane Rosenbaum), those looking forward and those looking back (Steve Stern), new immigrants from the Soviet Union (Gary Shteyngart and Lara Vapnyar) and every combination of the above.

At the same time, the generation of their elders (and their slightly elders), were still hard at work, many producing the best work of their careers, others still hoping that their best work would be yet to come.

Has there ever been a time like today, when American Jewish fiction writers have written on so many diverse subjects—while still writing "Jewish" fiction? One can read novel after novel and continually be surprised by the freshness of the individual visions.

That said, *Who We Are* at times feels like it is little more than those essays at the front of classics that you know you should read, but never do. Some fiction writers are not well suited to essay. Not all the essays in the collection are equally good, but surprises abound from writers who seem known, but really aren't, like Chaim Potok. And from writers that I know hardly at all, such as Johanna Kaplan, Stern or Lara Vapnyar, but am now anxious to read.

Perhaps all this discussion of American Jewish Fiction begs the question: Who cares?

How is it that these stories and novels appeal not only to Jewish readers, but also to readers of all faiths and all nationalities? Why does the Jewish experience in America, now 350 years old, continue to fascinate, to compel? And, equally, what compels these writers to set their visions down on paper?

Perhaps it is because we are the People of the Book. Perhaps it is our DNA, our fate, our curse, our story, to be witnesses, to document, to hear the stories and to tell the tales. Perhaps it is no coincidence that just as Joseph interpreted the dreams of the Pharaoh, Sigmund Freud decided truths could be found in the stories his patients told him of their dreams. Perhaps standing on a dais and, at age 13, reading in a foreign tongue and giving a little talk for one's bar or bat mitzvah can lead to a life of performing riffs. Perhaps the revenge of the child whose nose is stuck in a book, or excluded from some part of society, is to write stories, and seek approval in the form of publication.

Who We Are gives no definite answer. But whether one accepts or rejects the notion of being an American Jewish writer, what resonates is Singer's oft-quoted dictum that "Every writer must have an address."

What you do with who you are is, in the end, what it's all about.

November 24, 2005

CRYSTAL CLEAR

Billy Crystal has something he wants to share with you. Crystal has had a diverse and varied career, with plenty of ups and downs, as a stand-up comic, a TV performer and a movie actor. On the one hand, he starred in *When Harry Met Sally,* a movie that convinced many non-Jewish women to imagine that they were Meg Ryan and that they could find true happiness by sleeping with a short, funny Jew (we owe you big). On the other hand, there was *Rabbit Test* and *Father's Day,* which didn't do much for Crystal—or for me.

Crystal has done it all: He was a cast member in the heyday of *Saturday Night Live,* with his amazing impersonations of Fernando Lamas and Sammy Davis Jr.; he was on the short-lived but much-heralded sitcom, *Soap.* He's done every kind of movie, including action films, *Running Scared*; serious dramas, *Hamlet* and *Memories of Me*; huge box-office comedies, *Analyze This* and *City Slickers* and their sequels; a Woody Allen film, *Deconstructing Harry*; and animated films, most notably (at least in our home) *Monsters, Inc.*

But there was something Crystal had not done. No—not write a children's book. He's already done that (*I Already Know I Love You*).

What he had not done was really tell us about himself. About his childhood and the very special world he inhabited, all too briefly, with his father.

Crystal developed these stories into a one-man show, which he developed first at the La Jolla Playhouse and then took to Broadway as *700 Sundays*. The show has been not only a huge popular success; it was also a huge financial success on Broadway, a street littered with good intentions and poor investments. It even won a Tony Award, which Crystal accepted on the stage of Radio City Music Hall.

I would say that it doesn't get better than that. But it is evident that the best part for Crystal is performing *700 Sundays*. Crystal will perform *700 Sundays* in Los Angeles from Jan. 6 to Feb. 18 at the Wilshire Theatre. In the meantime, Warner Books has just published *700 Sundays* in book form.

I am not revealing any big secrets when I explain that Crystal's father, Jack, died when Crystal was 15. His father worked hard at two jobs, and the time they had together was mostly on Sundays—700 Sundays, Crystal once calculated.

Many of us never get over our childhoods (of such things do analysts and nostalgia merchants profit). Although childhood seems to pass slowly, even languidly at the time, and each memory is intense and heartfelt, all too soon it is a distant land that we strive to conjure up, recall and review in a new light of day.

In Crystal's case, his childhood was populated by some memorable characters—and some famous ones. Crystal's uncle was Milt Gabler. That name may not ring a bell (which is the point) but Gabler ran a record shop in Manhattan next to Grand Central Station called Commodore Records.

At one time, it was home base for the jazz world. Gabler not only sold records, found out-of-print records and re-issued them, but eventually he founded a record label. Crystal's father, Jack, became the store's manager and as a second job, organized concerts that he emceed.

This was no ordinary childhood. You go to the store, and Louis Armstrong is there, or Count Basie or Rosemary Clooney. The first movie Crystal ever saw was *Shane,* and the person who took him was Billie Holliday. Gabler produced and released *Strange Fruit* on his own label, when no one else would. Crystal called her Miss Billie, and she called him Mister Billy. That's something worth talking about.

One of the most touching scenes in the book is the jazz shiva that occurred spontaneously during the days following Crystal's father's death of a sudden heart attack. Crystal had shut himself in his room, unable to cry, not knowing how to mourn, when he heard large whoops coming from downstairs. His uncle, Bernhardt "Berns" Crystal, was telling stories, and then Wild Bill Davidson took out his horn and played some blues, and over the days that followed, 52nd Street relocated to Long Beach, Long Island, as Eddie Condon, Tyree Glenn, Zutty Singleton and others jammed a jazz farewell.

700 Sundays is also about that thing we all wonder about: How did we become who we've become? Crystal relates how on his fifth birthday he performed for a bunch of jazz musicians, and after they performed, he ran on stage and tap-danced. You get the impression that his fate was sealed then, and that, one way or another, he's been performing ever since.

He also talks about his passion for the Yankees and his veneration and eventual friendship with Mickey Mantle (and all without mentioning the fine HBO movie Crystal produced, "61").

In the book's acknowledgments, Crystal writes, "Creating and performing *700 Sundays* on Broadway was the most fulfilling time in my career."

It is easy to see why. What could be better than after a lifetime of playing roles, to write and perform work that tells people who you are—who you really are and what made you the way you are—and for the audience to appreciate it. Must be, in some small way, like writing *Tommywood.*

When I told my wife I was writing about *700 Sundays* in book form, she asked: "Does that mean we're not going to go see the show?" Let me tell you what I told her:

"Reading the book is like noshing on the appetizers. If you're not seeing *700 Sundays* in person, then you're just not getting Billy Crystal. It's the performance of a lifetime—his father's, his uncles', his aunts' and his. That, I want to see."

December 8, 2005

LARRY DAVID DIED FOR OUR SINS

Larry David, the producer-writer-star of *Curb Your Enthusiasm* has just finished airing the fifth season of his HBO program. Many people find him hilarious. Others find him annoying in the extreme. Both are right, of course, and David builds his humor out of this particular intersection of pain and pleasure. However, this season has been more than usually provocative, focusing on matters of identity—Jewish identity.

Curb has managed to offend all manner of Jews, from the observant to the assimilated. Arye Dworken, writing in the Jerusalem Post, had this to say:

"David not only makes fun of his own religion, he also makes up half of its customs, thereby misinforming viewers. His portrayal of Orthodox Jews...is reminiscent of the cartoons published by the Germans and French during World War II (the only thing missing were the grossly exaggerated noses)."

After pointing out inaccuracies and the extent to which David's Jewish characters are the ones with the show's worst behavior and character traits (angry, avaricious, foul-mouthed, neurotic, selfish), Dworken concludes, "I was saddened by David's obvious self-hatred and disrespect for his own tradition, but even sadder for the viewers who watch the show (albeit with a grain of salt) and are left with a false impression of Orthodoxy."

It is true *Curb* contains some inaccuracies and revels in many stereotypes, but as David suggested when accused in an early episode of being a self-loathing Jew. "'Self-loathing?' Yes. 'Jew?' Yes.' 'But Self-loathing Jew?' No."

Let me recap: At the beginning of this season, David was given reason to suspect he may have been adopted. His good friend, Richard Lewis, was in need of a kidney transplant, and much of the season dealt with whether Larry would donate his kidney. In the course of his ambivalence, Larry discovered that that the head of the kidney bank was an Orthodox Jew and, in an attempt to have Lewis rise up the donor list, David attempted to befriend him and his observant daughter. In the final episode of the season, David traveled to Arizona to meet his putative biological parents, the Cones, whom he discovered were not Jewish. This sent him into a paroxysm of changed behavior culminating in agreeing to donate his kidney. However, moments before surgery he learned he was not adopted and was, in fact, Jewish. Finally, David has his second near-death experience, the first of which had caused him to wonder why he was put on this earth.

Why, indeed.

I first met Larry David in 1980. He was appearing on *Fridays,* an ABC sketch-comedy program that hoped to do for the Sabbath eve what *Saturday Night* had accomplished for NBC's late night programming. I knew a woman who worked on the show. She was dating David. We hung out.

After the show's demise, David returned to New York where he worked briefly for *Saturday Night Live* and was writing screenplays that, as I recall, never made it out of the brown briefcase he carried with him.

One night I saw him take the stage at Catch a Rising Star, a New York comedy club. If memory serves me correctly, he wasn't on that long, and he ran off the stage. He was very funny. But the consensus was that he lacked an act—a stage persona—an identifiable, marketable shtick.

I remember standing one day in Times Square with David. Pointing to his briefcase, he said: "My problem is that I can only write what I write. I can't do anything else." Words that ring in my ear to this day (and every time I sit down at the computer).

Nonetheless, the reason that it was fun to hang out with David, and why, although at this point our conversations are limited to a once-a-year volley at the P.S. Arts benefit, it is still fun to talk to him—is that he has a special quality. Like the tennis pro who makes you feel you play better than you do, when you talk to Larry David you feel funnier, smarter, more confident, more convinced that you are entertaining to other people, David included.

So I wasn't surprised that Jerry Seinfeld, when offered the chance to create a pilot, turned to Larry to be his partner.

Seinfeld had a shtick, an identifiable persona, and he was incredibly affable and likeable. But you need a Larry David to convince you that your very conversations are what the show should be about.

Several years later, I visited David on the set of *Seinfeld*. He was gracious and welcoming and couldn't have been nicer. He confided that he was amazed by what was going on.

"I've never written a sitcom script in my life," he told me. "I have no idea how to do this."

Seinfeld's success is now in the history books. The combination of Seinfeld's charm and the neuroses of his castmates proved irresistible. *Seinfeld* was never a show about nothing, as has been much declaimed. The show began life as an exploration of how a comic comes up with his material, and morphed into how four profoundly selfish people mismanaged their personal lives in a way that bound them to each other.

Today, *Seinfeld* is in perpetual syndication, and there is many a night when I find myself revisiting Jerry's apartment or Monk's (easily recognizable as Tom's restaurant to Columbia grads and Upper-West Side denizens).

At a remove, I still marvel at the artistry of the comic performances, and the technical brilliance of those scripts that manage to bring together four separate plots into a jumble of escalating mayhem for the characters, leading to eventual disappointment, more often than not dismissed with a philosophical shrug.

One thing is different. Today, I can't help but feel the focus of my attention shifting from Jerry to George. Sure it's Jerry's show (after all it's called *Seinfeld,* not *Costanza*). But George is ...well, he's Larry David—without the success.

Curb Your Enthusiasm takes George and Larry David to a post-Seinfeld syndication-money world—a whole new level of the game. David has often explained that success has its limitations: People no longer think you have a right to complain. In fact, David, in a recent television special, explained that the only time anyone had felt sorry for him since he'd become wealthy was when he had a benign melanoma and there was a chance he might have had cancer.

In this season's final episode, David dies and goes to heaven where he suddenly has hair again. He is guided by two men with long white beards, dressed in robes, played by Dustin Hoffman and Sascha Baron Cohen. As if we didn't realize it already, they find Larry David so annoying that they send him back to live longer.

Yes it is true this season had many very Jewish moments: There was David buying scalped tickets for High Holiday services. There was an episode called, "The Seder," which had an adult guest cheating to find the afikomen and David refusing to pay the $1 prize. Yes, there was the Orthodox head of the kidney bank, and Izzy's Deli transformed into a sea of yarmulkes with David faking Yiddish by clearing his throat (too lazy and dismissive to even come up with the traditional fake Vos? Vos? Vos?"). There was David hiding the bacon, literally, from the Orthodox father and daughter. There was the daughter who, rather than be on a chair lift with David as the Sabbath came—jumps off (because there is no chance that David would). And there is that same daughter, with a surgically enhanced poitrine, done to improve her social appeal.

However, these all paled before the final episode. David travels to Arizona where he meets the couple he believes are his biological parents. The father looks somewhat like David, and they describe the adoptive parents they gave him up to as a couple who were nervous, made hand motions when they talked and that the woman dominated the man. To David, that sounds like the people who raised him.

He discovers that his biological parents are not Jewish and in an instant he changes: He goes to church, he rides horses, he fixes cars—he's a Jackie Mason caricature of a gentile. He returns home a different person: He wears sweater vests and jackets and ties. He goes to visit Richard Lewis and announces he is willing to give him his kidney. Lewis, who has a prominent mezuzah on his door, by contrast is (still) neurotic and unwilling to loan David his golf clubs. But David embraces him nonetheless. After he leaves, Lewis mutters, "Jesus Christ."

As he's being wheeled into surgery, David discovers that he is, in fact, Jewish. Upon his recovery, he's asked if he has any cause to reconsider anything in his life—a montage of his worst moments flashes before his (and our) eyes. It is a cavalcade of ungracious, insulting and selfish behavior. Having reviewed them, David decides he wouldn't change a thing. He's back to being Larry David.

What are we to conclude? That Jews are hysterical, mean, selfish, brutish, unattractive louts while non-Jews are reasonable, well-dressed empaths full of love and forgiveness?

If you do, then you've missed the point.

Larry David, the real one, not the TV Larry David, is married and has kids. He is charitable and engaged in causes. Publicly he blames this on his wife, Laurie, but the truth is that whether or not you agree with their politics or choices, they have put their considerable talents and financial resources in the service of causes they believe in—when they don't have to, when they could choose to live like—well, like David on *Curb Your Enthusiasm.*

Remember how I said that David's weakness as a stand-up performer was that he lacked a shtick? Well, the David of *Curb Your Enthusiasm* has one: He's Larry David, self-proclaimed "Radical Narcissist."

The David of *Curb* is the world's most selfish man. As such he sees every person as the embodiment of a stereotype—and rates them only by what they have to offer him, or to the extent he can avoid extending himself to them. This man can not appreciate why Orthodox practice would have meaning to a young woman, anymore than he can understand why someone would want to lead you on a tour of their house. It just doesn't interest him.

This David is funny, much as George Costanza was funny, because we understand him. We, too, on occasion, are selfish. We, too, on occasion, stereotype and think less of others.

The David of *Curb* may not be the best person, but that makes him neither a bad Jew, nor bad for the Jews. To single him out as representative of all Jews is to indulge in the sort of stereotyping typical of Larry David himself.

Which brings me to my final point: The Larry David of *Curb Your Enthusiasm* is not the anti-Christ or a Jewish anti-Semite. To the contrary, this season, David is supposed to have died and been reborn just like that wunderkind from Nazareth, Jesus.

Let me then put forward the argument that David has a higher purpose: He makes us laugh not only because his behavior is so outrageous, but also because it does him so little good. When he scalps High Holiday synagogue tickets, he is thrown out by a security guard. His attempt to suck up to the head of the kidney bank fails. Even when he goes to heaven, they find him too annoying.

David is here to ask us to "curb our enthusiasm," to show us that there is no joy in a shallow life of radical narcissism. That if we want to find meaning in our lives, if we want better relationships with our friends and our spouses, we should laugh at him, but not live like him.

Or just think of it this way: Larry David died for our sins.

December 24, 2005

FIGHT OF THE CENTURY

Joe Louis' boxing match against Max Schmeling at Yankee Stadium in 1938 remains one of the great sporting events of the twentieth century—even though the fight in front of nearly 70,000 spectators lasted all of two minutes and four seconds.

Some sixty-seven years after that fateful night of fisticuffs, David Margolick, a *Vanity Fair* contributing editor and former New York Times staffer, has written the authoritative account of a time when the fate of nations seemed to hang in the balance of one boxing match. *Beyond Glory* (Knopf, 2005) is a book that Margolick describes as "so Jewish"—even if its protagonists were not.

Margolick's journey to write this book started, he said, when he was eight or nine and his father played "I Can Hear It Now," an Edward R. Murrow/Fred Friendly recording that featured Clem McCarthy calling the second Louis-Schmeling fight. Schmeling had won their first bout—and as the rematch approached, it seemed as if the men in the ring were stand-ins for a fight between Nazi supremacy and American democracy.

Many years later, as the twentieth century passed into the twenty-first, Margolick was surprised to find there was no book on the subject. Margolick realized that in Joe Louis and Max Schmeling, he had two great stories that provided "a natural architecture, almost like a double helix, as they chased each other and met."

At the same time, the story encompasses the sport of boxing in its glory days, during a moment in time when two men's personal dramas enthralled the nation and the world. *Beyond Glory* is an account of the 1930s—"the fateful decade" as Margolick called it. Unavoidably and inevitably, *Beyond Glory* is also the story of race relations in the United States and of Hitler's rise to power in Germany.

Margolick has created this historical page-turner, weighing in at 351 pages, the old-fashioned way: with exhaustive research in archives and on microfilm in libraries all over the world. He has amassed a Himalaya of detail, distilling it seamlessly into a cohesive, compelling narrative that takes the reader from the boxing ring to the streets of Harlem, to cities in the North and South of the United States and even into Goebbel's living room, where Schmeling's wife listened to the fight with the Nazi leader and his spouse.

In the mid-1960s, Truman Capote famously applied the techniques of fiction to reporting *In Cold Blood,* and as the film, *Capote,* tells us, "he changed the way nonfiction was written." There is no question that many have followed down that road—writing in a style that delivers a breathless you-are-there quality.

Margolick, by contrast, is old school: He gives the readers the facts and lets them draw their own conclusions. "Beyond Glory" is not the story of what Margolick thinks; it is an account of what others witnessed. Margolick's love for his subject and respect for each detail is evident in his meticulous account.

Margolick's approach is informed by his training as a newspaper reporter, as well as his background as an attorney, and by his experience writing about judges, lawyers and cases as the former *At the Bar* columnist for *The New York Times.* (In that capacity, Margolick was responsible for my own 15 minutes of fame, when he profiled me as an attorney-turned-author of a book about the Demjanjuk trial in Israel).

In person, Margolick conveys strong opinions about Louis and Schmeling. For example, he feels Louis' impact on civil rights in America is largely forgotten because, by the 1960s, he was regarded as a retro Uncle Tom figure.

"People had forgotten," Margolick says, "what a colossally important cultural figure he was." He also feels that Louis' victory against Schmeling was a touchstone in American Jews' identification with the plight of African Americans—way before the civil rights movement.

In *Beyond Glory*, Schmeling comes across as shrewd, a boxer who properly assessed Louis' weaknesses in their first fight in 1936, to beat him. This shrewdness also showed outside the ring, where Schmeling cultivated the good will of the Nazi leadership, without ever joining the Nazi party. And after the war, he smartly maneuvered to receive the German Coca-Cola franchise that made him a millionaire. He would live long enough to be perceived in post-war Germany as an athletic icon.

History was kind to Schmeling: Over the years, he wrote three autobiographies without risking his reputation to a competing serious biography. His post-war renown also was enhanced by a curious twist of fate. On Kristallnacht, Schmeling protected two young Jewish children, brothers, who were his neighbors. They survived and prospered, and years later, Henri

Lewin, now a Los Angeles resident and successful Las Vegas casino owner, was alive to speak of Schmeling's act of courage.

Still, Margolick felt the true, entire story of Schmeling had not been told. Margolick tried in vain to meet and interview Schmeling (who died Feb. 2, 2005, at age ninety-nine), even going so far as to travel to Germany and knock on his door, only to be rebuffed.

For the record, Margolick judges Schmeling more harshly in person than the book does. In Margolick's estimation, Schmeling, although loyal to Jews he knew personally, during the war years showed "microcourage and macrocowardice."

Margolick faults Schmeling for never speaking out against what was happening in Germany. Margolick makes the case that Schmeling could easily have lived in the United States, could have led his career here—many non-Jewish Germans did, including Marlene Dietrich. In the end, Margolick sees Schmeling as symbolizing all Germany, where average and not-so-average Germans individually and collectively allowed evil to thrive, even as they were willing to prosper in its midst.

In this way, *Beyond Glory* is in Margolick's estimation, "a Jewish book because it's about civil rights, a natural Jewish affinity between blacks and Jews. It's a book about Nazism, about Hitler's rise and about how one boxer reacted to it." Furthermore, as Margolick told me, "Boxing was a Jewish enterprise. Half of the people in the seats were Jews." The promoters, the managers, the trainers, the writers were mostly Jews.

However, the fundamental reason that *Beyond Glory* should be considered a Jewish book is because any book Margolick writes is inevitably Jewish.

In his omnivorous research, Margolick read the Yiddish papers, which normally didn't cover sports but covered this.

And not only the Yiddish papers but the Polish Yiddish papers (which the Yiddishist Eddy Portnoy helped him with) and the Polish Jewish newspapers (read by assimilated Polish Jews). It was there that Margolick found a poem that appears in the book, written by Wladyslaw Szengel, a Polish Jew living in Warsaw:

Hey Louis! You probably don't know
What your punches meant to us
You, in anger, punched the Brown Shirts
Straight in their hearts—K.O.

Szengel's fate in Poland can only be imagined; Margolick said he was especially proud to include the poem: "It brought back to life this man's voice."

Who else would include that poem in a book about the Schmeling-Louis fight?

January 5. 2006

COMEDY MATTERS

"After 9/11, all I did was sit around and be scared," Albert Brooks told me recently. "After a year and a half," Brooks now says, "I just got tired of it."

He wondered, "Why isn't this being processed? Do we never mention it?" Looking at what Hollywood was releasing to the public, he concluded that "most of the [current] movies take place in the past—or are teenage sex comedies."

Brooks decided to do something about it. His response, *Looking for Comedy in the Muslim World,* which opened in Los Angeles on January 20, imagines that a U.S. government commission contacts Albert Brooks (not their first choice, but he's available) to travel to India and Pakistan to better understand the Muslim mind. They've tried bombing and spying, argues lawyer-actor, senator-actor Fred Dalton Thompson who's leading the commission, why not explore comedy?

The movie opens with Brooks auditioning for Penny Marshall for the lead role in a remake of *Harvey.* The scene is played perfectly and succinctly illustrates the humiliation that attends working in Hollywood.

So when offered the chance to do "important" work—and possibly earn the Medal of Freedom—he signs on.

When Brooks goes to India, he is at first flummoxed by the challenge of how to find out what people think is funny there. Apparently, there are no comedy clubs in New Delhi, so he decides to stage a comedy concert.

Of course, as Brooks pointed out in our conversation, if the U.S. government actually wanted to find out about humor on the Indian subcontinent, it would never send a comic. And as I pointed out to Brooks, if a comic wanted to find out what Indians thought was funny, he might show them a whole range of classic comedy, say a smidgen of Chaplin, some Keaton, maybe a soupcon of Lucy and a smattering of the Three Stooges, some Richard Pryor, some Seinfeld, some Chris Rock—rather than performing a revue of some of his own greatest hits—which is exactly what Brooks does.

And that, folks, is part of the joke. Brooks has always mined comedy that operates at several levels, including deconstructing comedy itself.

Brooks, nee Einstein (yes, that's a fact) is the son of actress-singer Thelma Leeds and Harry Einstein. Einstein was a comedian who performed as Parkyakarkus on the Al Jolson and Eddie Cantor radio shows. He died on stage, literally, after completing a performance at the Friar's Club when Albert was 11—an event that shaped Brooks' worrying persona, and his comic one as well.

Brooks was famously funny even at Beverly Hills High. After graduating, he pursued acting but found success performing comedy.

Brooks appeared on the *Ed Sullivan Show* and the *Tonight Show* doing wild cerebral bits, ventriloquists who spoke more than their dummies, mimes who described their every gesture, animal tricks lacking the right animal. Brooks never tried out these bits—as legend has it and as he confirmed in our conversation—he just went on stage and performed them.

During the first season of *Saturday Night Live,* he made several short films that became comedy classics. A few years later, he began making his own feature films.

In the 1979 *Real Life,* he played "Albert Brooks," who decides to make a documentary about an American family (like the Louds on PBS) and who is so bored by them he interferes to create a "better" show—presaging all that has followed in so-called reality TV.

In *Modern Romance* (1981), Brooks dissected a breakup; in *Lost in America* (1985), he took apart a couple who decide to ditch life in Los Angeles to discover America and themselves; in *Defending Your life"* (1991), he tackled the afterlife; in *Mother* (1996), his character decides that he can't have a successful relationship until he resolves his relationship with his mother (played by Debbie Reynolds), and in *The Muse* (1999), he explored creativity and the writer's life.

Now, with his latest film, *Looking for Comedy in the Muslim World,* Brooks has decided to deconstruct Albert Brooks himself. The conceit of the film is that Brooks' ego as a comedian is such that he is seduced by the thought he might contribute to world peace; that even though he is most well known as someone who voiced a fish in an animated movie, when he puts on a show, it is of all his own material.

And when he bombs, he doesn't accept it as a failure—just a matter of the show having been scheduled for too early a crowd. His vindication comes when he crosses into Pakistan and performs for a group of would-be stand-up comics who find his work hilarious, perhaps because it's funny, perhaps because they've all been smoking hashish. In the end, there is no medal, and he has nearly caused an international incident, but he is hailed by his friends and family as "our hero."

At the same time, we, as an audience, get to see Brooks do his ventriloquist routine and his improv routine—bits he has not performed in decades.

It is as if Brooks is saying: "This is who I am; this is what I do," and that, despite the ways in which the world, and Hollywood in particular, belittles the sort of comedy Brooks is interested in, he has to go on doing it. It's important.

It is also about Brook's own existential search for meaning—to prove that after September 11, what he does matters.

When I told Brooks this, he said: "Yes."

I prodded him to elaborate.

"There's no movie that's going to change the world," Brooks acknowledged.

However, Brooks maintains that "laughter is one of the best lubricants." To Brooks, laughter is healing; laughter is survival.

"It's not just car exhaust," Brooks told me. "You're adding things to the atmosphere. It goes somewhere."

I told him that I thought *Looking for Comedy* was his personal *Sullivan's Travels,* a classic Preston Sturges film about a director who discovers the value of comedy films.

"OK," Brooks responded.

Frankly, I was hoping for a more expansive answer—something about the existential dilemma we all face that can be all the more acute when confronting life in Hollywood—and the importance of finding satisfaction in what we do. But, "OK" will do.

Or as Brooks put it more simply: "Comedy matters."

January 26, 2006

THE GETTY VILLA

THE WOW! FACTOR

Before me sat a poet, flanked on each side by his muses. Was this Orpheus himself? His lyre was missing, and he looked off in the distance. Were the muses there to inspire him, or perhaps, to inspire me?

No, this was not just another late night of hanging out with Mary Kate and Ashley and one of their glazed-eyed rocker beaus—on this mid-morning my tastes were more classical: I was touring the newly restored Getty Villa in Pacific Palisades, which opened to the public on Jan. 28.

To cut to the chase: The Getty Villa is magnificent, wonderful, in short, as my daughter said after jet skiing for the first time: "It was totally awesome." First, a bit of history: J. Paul Getty was an oil scion, born in Minneapolis in 1892, who attended USC and Berkeley and graduated Oxford in 1914. He made his first million by 1916 and retired in 1917 to become a Hollywood playboy—but like so many careers in Hollywood, it was no way to live, so he returned to business. As founder of Getty Oil, he became one the world's first billionaires. He wrote a book called, *How to Be Rich,* which, as the title indicates, is different from how to become rich.

In 1945, Getty purchased a sixty-four acre site in Pacific Palisades, and less than a decade later built the J. Paul Getty Museum to exhibit his expanding collection of Old Master paintings and sculptures, many of which were antiquities. In 1968, Getty got the idea of recreating a Roman country house as home for his collections, choosing as his inspiration the Villa dei Papiri, a first century Roman country house in Herculaneum that was buried, along with Pompeii, by the eruption of Mt. Vesuvius in 79 C.E.

Although the Roman villa was only ever partially excavated, and remains buried to this day, engineers had drawn a putative map of the property, and these became the basis for Getty's villa.

The Getty museum opened in 1974. There was some controversy at the time over the whole notion of "recreating" a villa—an act of appropriation replete with a lack of authenticity one might deride as a rich man's whim. Over time, the objections became more muted. Getty died in 1976, and the museum continued to be an important Southern California art destination until 1997, when it was closed for renovation—six months before the opening of the new Getty on the hills above Brentwood and the 405 Freeway.

In case you never visited the Palisades Getty in its prior incarnation, you used to enter via elevator right into the building. The rooms were dark and stuffy. There was no good way to get from the first to second floor, except by a narrow staircase. In order to protect some of the artworks from the light, there were few windows if any. What people remembered most about the

Getty Villa were its gardens, a peristyle around a pool, as well as the little cafe in the back where one could have tea. That, and the complicated reservation and parking arrangement.

What a difference a $275 million renovation makes.

One now arrives to a cobblestone street and an imposing portico. This allows you to look down the canyon and out to the sea. You also get a good view of the mansion below it, the Villa Leon, which is the classical building one sees from the Pacific Coast Highway that many mistake for the Getty but which is a private home that has been on the market for many years. From the portico or from the parking garage of the villa, you take a path along a walkway carved into the side of the canyon, leading to "the arrival balcony," part of a calculated strategy by Boston-based architects Rodolfo Machado and Jorge Silvetti to deliver a "Wow!" moment.

Wow! Indeed. As you turn the corner, you are dazzled by a 180-degree panorama that looks over the roof of the villa itself, down the canyon and out to the sea. You can take in the breadth of the outdoor peristyle gardens, the new entrance of the Getty Villa in all its classical splendor, and then look up the hill to the new structures, the cafe (you order the food and they bring it out to you) with indoor and outdoor seating and a snack cart, as well as a new museum gift shop, the Getty ranch house and the new buildings devoted to staff, conferences, conservation and education.

In this way the architects have surrounded the restored Getty Villa with new buildings engaging in a dialogue between new and old, just as the villa itself engages in a dialogue between interior and exterior and a conversation between the classical form of a Roman home and the high-tech state-of-the-art installation of the holdings inside.

What Machado and Silvetti have done is to make of the villa itself an object of art to be contemplated and appreciated—something that never happened in the prior incarnation. This is also a nod to the Getty Center whose building and gardens have become the stars as much, if not more, than the collections inside.

Also attached to the new Getty Villa is a 250-seat indoor theater, as well as several classrooms. All this and we haven't even entered the villa yet.

Get ready for another "Wow" moment: You enter into an atrium which leads into the inner peristyle, and flows to a new grand staircase, framing a view of the colorful mosaic fountain in the east garden.

Now for the art: The Getty will feature some 1,200 items from its collection of approximately 44,000 objects spanning 6,500 B.C.E. to the 10th century C.E. I can't tell you whether what remains in storage outshines what is presented; or if only exhibiting a small fraction of them is a disappointment. But I can say that what is showcased is done in a very aesthetically pleasing manner.

The twenty-three galleries, once organized chronologically, are now grouped by themes. The ground floor features rooms devoted to gods and goddesses, mythological monsters and heroes (including art devoted to stories from the Trojan War), a basilica and a room devoted to the Temple of Herakles, which features a gorgeous and intricately patterned mosaic floor. It is here you will find Orpheus, along with Zeus, Hera and Apollo, all looking better than ever (this is Los Angeles; assume they've had work done).

I regret to report that you will not be attending weddings in the basilica, or dancing the hora in the amphitheater. Due to the restrictive covenants under which the Getty operates, as well agreements made with the neighbors, the Getty Villa will not be available for private family and social functions.

However, families and children of all ages will certainly enjoy two rooms on the ground floor: "the family forum," a kid-friendly art room, where children can shadow-play and decorate vases, thereby learning about the forms and variety of Greek vases, as well as "the Timescape room," a clever interactive exhibit that places the Getty Villa and its holdings of Greek, Roman and Etruscan art in historical context.

One of the architectural challenges facing Machado and Silvetti was the flow from ground floor to the second level. To this end they designed a grand staircase—it is their artistic flourish, their own signature piece in the Getty Villa.

The first thing one appreciates on the second floor is the light. The upstairs now has fifty-eight more windows and three new skylights (one of which, above the atrium, can be opened), as well as several accessible terraces.

The galleries focus on life in the ancient world, men, women, sports, coins and jewelry. My favorite was the amphora given to winners of athletic competitions, as well as the ceramics depicting the competitions themselves.

There are also five galleries for changing exhibitions. The first three exhibitions to be shown at the Getty are: *Antiquity and Photography,* featuring early photos of the Parthenon and the Sphinx, as well as some of the earliest Daguerrotypes; *The Getty Villa Reimagined,* which looks at the models and designs which led to the current renovation, and *Glassmaking in Antiq-*

uity, which features highlights from the recently acquired Oppenlander glass collection which features beautiful exemplars of Jerusalem glass.

One of the most impressive aspects of the Getty Villa is the display. The rooms are painted in colors that suggest the classical world yet complement the holdings presented. No room feels overcrowded. The cases, many of which have built-in stabilizers for earthquake protection, are placed at a comfortable eye level.

Machado and Silvetti also designed the mosaic floors in the galleries and which are graceful and at the same time whimsical.

Even as I give credit where credit is due both to architects and to acting curator Carole Wright, I wonder: What is it about Greco-Roman and Etruscan antiquities that compels our attention?

Part of it is a worship of and curiosity about the great cultures that came before us. Part of it is a fascination with objects that carried great import to past societies. Or that reveal life in ancient times. The reach of the Greek and Roman empires extended throughout Europe, North Africa, the Middle East and parts of Asia, and as such can be seen as the cradle from which much of Western culture sprung.

But more than any of the above, there is a beauty we recognize in Greco-Roman antiquities that touches us even today. Much of modern art has been about, as Robert Hughes dubbed it, "the shock of new."

And while much of modern art has focused on dissonance and cutting through the clutter, ancient art speaks of harmony.

Part of what is so pleasing about the Getty Villa is that the building itself and the gardens are, like the Greco-Roman art it displays, all about proportion. The interplay of interior and exterior, the sight lines and the vistas, the columns and the height of the rooms, even the space afforded in most galleries relative to the number of items exhibited, all contrive to give pleasure from harmonious proportions.

As I toured the Getty Villa, I also pondered the intersection of Hellenism and Judaism. As you are probably aware, when Alexander the Great conquered the Middle East, in the fourth century B.C.E., he allowed the Jewish people great freedoms and the right to practice their religion. As a result, many Jewish parents began naming their children Alexander, a tradition that continues today in all its international variants such as Xander, Sandor and Sasha.

For several centuries, Jews continued to thrive under Greek leaders. The Torah was translated into Greek (some claim the translation was for the Great Library in Alexandria and was from the Aramaic before there was even a Hebrew version). Some claim that seventy-two scholars were assembled to compile it. In any event, there is lore to the effect that Greek is a language especially pleasing to the Hebrew deity.

Although Babylonia may have been the first Jewish exile community, it was among the Greeks that assimilation first became an issue (so much so that in those days Jews called assimilation "Hellenism").

The complaints may sound familiar: Jews were forgetting the ways of their forefathers. They could no longer read, write or speak Hebrew—having turned to Greek instead. They were not observing the commandments, and could no longer say the prayers. The Sabbath was not being observed: Worse yet, young men were engaging in athletics on the Sabbath, throwing the discus or participating in wrestling competitions (the rabbis were particularly offended that wrestling was in the nude; but my guess is that the Jewish mothers weren't so crazy about all that fighting). There was even a reform movement led by rabbis, Jewish philosophers and Jews practicing new forms of Greek-leavened Judaism.

To many, it was a golden age. The Greeks were an intellectual society who venerated the old but appreciated youth; they were intellectual yet hedonistic. Jews began to flourish in society. But alas, assimilation, as manifested through its expression in a succession of societies to present time, has often charted a historical trajectory, much like that of Icarus, of exaltation and exhilaration followed by bad news and worse news.

As our young Chanukah scholars will tell you—Hellenism reached its nadir for Jews when Antiochus IV banned Judaism in the second century B.C.E., and insisted Jews worship the Greek Gods. A further blow followed when the Maccabees, Jewish zealots, successful in their revolt against the Greeks and Syrians, put to death those fellow Jews whom they found not sufficiently observant.

Which brings me back to the Getty Villa. Part of the terrible beauty we see in antiquities is the knowledge that the societies that created them are no more. Their gods and their beauty could not protect them from the inexorable march of fate. Whether as per Robert Frost's formulation, you side with ice or fire, or per the Greeks with the Hedonists or the Stoics, or in our times with the observant or the assimilated of all faiths, the Getty Villa has reopened in the Palisades to allow us to appreciate the beauty that Greco-Roman culture gave us, both fleeting and lasting. Not only that, now you can also grab a bite at the cafe, and buy a memento mori at the museum store.

February 2, 2006

SAYINGS OF CHAIRMAN LEVINE

"When is a dirty bathroom a broken window?" This is the question that opens Michael Levine's recently published business tome, *Broken Windows, Broken Business* (Warner Business Books).

Levine is a successful Hollywood publicist. I am indebted to him forever for one of my most memorable *Tommywood* moments—a séance with Hollywood's evergreen legend, Robert Evans, at his home, and on his bed (see *The Kid Still Stays in the Picture,* March 2004).

Levine, like many a Hollywood success story, is self-made.

Born in New York City, Levine graduated from Fort Lee High in 1972, and attended Rutgers College for six months. At eighteen, with no job and, in his words, "a home life under an alcoholic mother," he was determined to forge a life of his own invention.

Levine had a passion for the entertainment industry and began his show business career as an impresario, renting out the local movie theater in New Jersey on weekends after the last show and putting on midnight screenings of *Reefer Madness* and other cult movies.

In 1977, Levine arrived in Los Angeles looking for work in movie promotion. By 1983 he had opened his own firm.

"The most difficult thing is to get your first client," Levine told me over tea at the Beverly Wilshire. He said it was "like trying to staple jelly to the ceiling."

His first clients were Joan Rivers and David Brenner. Steve Reidman, Brenner's then manager (now a beloved fourth-grade public school teacher in Toluca Lake) recalls that Levine's devotion to his clients was 24/7.

"One advantage I had," Levine recalled recently, "was that I was entering the business at a time of change...[the business then] was mostly old white guys. I was more intense."

He still is.

Over the years he has represented a smorgasbord of talent, everyone from Demi Moore to David Bowie, as well as Prince, Kareem, Jon Voigt, Cameron Diaz, Jon Stewart, Dave Chappell, Ozzy Osbourne, Suzanne Somers and even the gloved one, Michael Jackson. He repped Barbra Streisand when she returned to Las Vegas and Nancy Kerrigan when she was attacked by Tonya Harding.

Recently, Levine relinquished the title of president to longtime associate Dawn Miller. He retains the title of chairman. However, giving up some day-to-day management affords Levine the opportunity to pursue other interests—and to express his theories.

Broken Windows applies to business the theories on controlling crime that were put forth by professors James Q. Wilson and George L. Kelling and applied, most notably, in New York by Mayor Rudy Giuliani and Police Commissioner William Bratton, who is now LA's police chief. Levine paints a convincing picture that businesses need to pay attention to those areas where they intersect with their consumers—first impressions matter, as do all the details that make up that first impression: the business representatives the consumer interfaces with, their attitude, the environment where that intersection takes place (store, Web site, phone conversation). All the small details contribute to whether the consumer will conclude a sale and continue to do business with one vendor over another. The book is about "how the smallest remedies reap the biggest rewards."

Levine decries a business culture where the incompetent get reassigned rather than fired.

"Businesses don't understand that little things matter a lot," he says.

Which brings us back to those broken windows. Repairing them makes a difference.

All very sensible and practical.

As for our conversation...My mother had a saying: "Everyone in the world is crazy, except you and me. And sometimes I wonder about you."

Clearly, Levine is successful; he is charming and he is wily. "Broken Windows" is his seventeenth book.

I wondered if Levine is, as Oudom, my Cambodian-born nephew might say, "a bissele meshugah." (I taught him that!)

You decide. Here are some of the sayings of Chairman Levine:

1. "Most people are motivated by three things: 1) Cash; 2) Love and Sex; 3) Fame and Power—if you can deliver one, you're doing OK, but if you can deliver more than one, you are going to get their attention."

2. How do you get your first client? "Somehow."

3. On motivation: "If you've got a gun in your mouth, you'll do anything."

4. "[There are] two pieces to our brain: the logical and the emotional. Eighty percent of the time, emotion wins out. [However] when the human is hungry, angry, lonely or tired—then emotion wins 100 percent of the time."

5. "The central question of life is: What do you most want, and what are you willing to give up to get it?"

Levine dismisses the notion of "balance."

"No one achieves supersuccess in life," he says, "without some part of their life suffering...Something's got to give."

As for the culture of celebrity and the publicity-mad world Levine has toiled in, he remarks that in America we have a "more and more sophisticated culture, but a less reverent society."

"Once upon a time, achievement preceded fame. Think of Jonas Salk," Levine says.

But today fame precedes achievement (Think: Paris Hilton).

The reason: "Technology is the principal difference," Levine says. "Technology is the enemy of reverence."

Again I ask: who thinks like this? Michael Levine does. To paraphrase George Bernard Shaw: Some men (like me) see a broken window, and it is just a broken window, and others (like Levine) see a broken window and see a way to fix a business—and write a book.

February 16, 2006

A WORLD OF MUSIC

A few weeks ago, the Paris-based world music ensemble Les Yeux Noirs performed at Royce Hall as part of UCLA Live. Led by brothers Olivier and Eric Slabiak, violin virtuosos who are the Paris-born grandchildren of Polish Jewish immigrants, Les Yeux Noirs played improvisations on Russian, Yiddish, Romanian and Roma songs, as well as their own eclectic compositions (including one that puts Baudelaire's poem "Invitation au Voyage" to music.). What a trip it was!

This concert just confirmed a feeling I've had for some time: Even if Los Angeles is not the center of the world—as I sometimes believe it is—the city has increasingly become a center for world music.

This spring you can attend amazing performances all over LA: Le Mystère des Voix Bulgares are performing at Disney Hall on March 8; Césaria Évora, the nightingale of Cape Verde, plays at Royce Hall on March 17; Pierre Bensusan, the French Algerian guitar maestro of Sephardic heritage plays at the Skirball on March 30. And that's before summer programs kick in at the Hollywood Bowl's world music series, as well as the sunset concerts on the Santa Monica Pier and Grand Performances, the series of free world music concerts held downtown.

There is no easy definition for what constitutes world music. Generally speaking, we are referring to music made in second- or third-world countries. Often we are talking about music made by non-Europeans in languages other than English—but even that is not always the case. Nor is world music a code word for the primitive rhythms of indigenous people—it can as easily refer to complex modulations of Latin or East Asian music. World music can be the music of longing, of exile, or the expression of joy, or the joyous expression of a spiritual rapture.

There are many portals to world music. Many listeners I know first encountered it through the reggae of Bob Marley, or the African beats of King Sunny Ade or Fela Kuti; others began their journey in Brazil with a girl from Ipanema, a samba or some smooth bossa nova. In Los Angeles, one can travel via radio to Tom Schnabel's *Cafe LA* (www.kcrw.org) or to Yatrika Shah-Rais' *Global Village* on KPFK Pacifica radio (www.kpfk.org). And for those still buying CDs, now that Rhino Westwood and Hatikvah Records have passed from the scene, all roads lead to the world music section of Amoeba Music in Hollywood, which has one of the most extensive offerings.

For myself, I can trace no specific moment of initiation; no Ur moment. Was it the Csardas or some Roma music that I heard in some Hungarian restaurant as a child? Or perhaps the cymbalom-driven theme to *The Third Man*? Was I made a devotee after Ravi Shankar's appearance at the "Concert for Bangladesh"? Or was I entranced by a late-night show of Jimmy Cliff's "The Harder They Come"? Was it the summer I spent in Brazil after my high school graduation? Or maybe it was afternoons at my uncle Emil's, when he would excitedly play a cassette of some obscure Eastern European cantor so I could hear some long-lost niggun (wordless melody) he'd uncovered.

My best guess is "Answer D: All of the above."

For whatever the reason, all I know is that world music has a strange power over me—it takes me out of myself to places I want to go, while at the same time making me feel at home.

World music, as its name indicates, belongs to all people of the world. But it seems to attract people who can hear the universal in the particular.

So if the question is "Who is responsible for the explosion of world music in LA?" The answer is more people than you can imagine. David Sefton does a great job at UCLA Live, and Michael Alexander is to be commended for the Grand Performances at California Plaza. But for this article, I would like to highlight two people who deserve special mention: The aforementioned Tom Schnabel and Yatrika Shah-Rais. Schnabel has probably introduced more people in LA to world music over the years than anyone else; and then there's Shah-Rais, who made the Skirball Cultural Center into a world music destination.

Schnabel seems, at first meeting, an unlikely avatar of world music. As he recounted recently over lunch, he is California born and bred; he grew up in Santa Monica Canyon, attended Pali High, was a surfer and worked summers as a lifeguard at Dockweiler Beach. You'd imagine his passion would be for Jan and Dean or Dick Dale. However, at sixteen he heard John Coltrane's "Impressions," and it was, in his words, "a mystical experience." He became a jazz aficionado, listening to 105.1 KBCA. Schnabel attended USC, where his passion for jazz led to an interest in classical music, Debussy in particular.

He then went to France, where he taught English. It was there that he first heard African and Arab music and began his lifelong passion for world music. However, after breaking up with his French girlfriend, he returned to Los Angeles. He tried to get a teaching job here, but couldn't find any. In an attempt to create a new life, one more involved with music, he started to write liner notes for Downbeat magazine, and he started doing a radio show on KCRW.

"Everything just coalesced," he says.

On July 19, 1979, Schnabel became musical director of KCRW (a position he held until 1990): "I was in the right place at the right time."

Reggae and African music were becoming popular. In the 1980s, Los Angeles was home to several clubs that supported African music.

"It was fun," he recalls.

I remember visiting Los Angeles during that period and being taken to a club that stood somewhere in the shadow of the 10 and 405 freeways, where a sweating King Sunny Ade invited the frenzied crowd to leap on stage, dance with him and stick dollar bills to his forehead.

Schnabel also hosted *Morning Becomes Eclectic* throughout the 1980s, until he ceded the show to Chris Douridas (the program is now hosted by Nic Harcourt). During Schnabel's tenure, the list of world music artists he was the first to play would be too long to cite.

Says Schnabel: "World music is honest music. The lyrics mean something. There's a lot of virtuosity."

At one point, Schnabel became a "suit," working for A&M, where he had his own label. Schnabel is responsible for one of my favorite albums *A Meeting by the River*, the collaboration between Ry Cooder and Vishwa Mohan Bhatt.

At this point in his illustrious career, Schnabel is a man of many business cards. He hosts *Cafe LA* on KCRW (Sunday noon-2 p.m.); he is program director of world music for the LA Phil, programming shows at Disney Hall, as well as the Hollywood Bowl; and he continues to do music consulting and supervision.

In the coming months he is hosting programs at Disney Hall, such as Mônica Salmaso, Les Ballets Africans and Ravi Shankar. This summer, the Hollywood Bowl World Music series will feature a Sergio Mendes evening, a Bollywood evening and a reggae night, as well as other acts still to be announced.

Schnabel has great respect for his colleagues programming world music in LA He feels they are people who have great heart, citing the wonderful shows Grand Performances puts on for free and describing Shah-Rais, at the Skirball Center as "a beautiful person inside and out."

Katrika Shah-Rais was born in Iran and educated in France. She has degrees in international relations and has worked for environmental and human rights organizations. Before coming to the Skirball, she worked at a management and booking agency and at the World Music Institute in New York.

Although she grew up a Beatles and rock music fan, in many ways it is her background in international relations that draws her to world music. Music, she told me recently, "is the best tool to bring people together."

Shah-Rais came to the Skirball in 1998. With the Skirball's support, she has made the center, whose nominal mission was to explore the connections between Jewish heritage and America into, in her words, "a gathering place where an exchange of ideas and culture takes place."

By using its three venues (an auditorium, an outside plaza and the Ahmanson Hall) the Skirball can cater to audiences as small as a few hundred or as large as 800 (which is still small by concert standards). However, having this flexibility has allowed Shah-Rais and the Skirball to feature lesser-known artists and build an audience for them and their counterparts.

In recent months, the Skirball has featured jazz musician Ben Sidran and Czech Songwriter Maria Topferova. Coming up are guitarist Pierre Bensusan on March 30 and singer songwriter Keren Ann on May 11.

What struck me about my conversations with both Schnabel and Shah-Rais was that they both see music in general, and world music in particular, as a way to educate and bring people together.

"World music is a gateway," Schnabel told me, "it expands you."

Or, as Shah-Rais told me, "The common language is music."

World music faces many challenges. Given the current geo-political situation, getting visas for foreign artists can be time consuming and difficult—for example, very few Cuban artists currently are being allowed to perform in the United States. At the same time, some foreign artists, resentful of the U.S. procedures are themselves less interested in performing here than in, say, Europe or Latin America.

Also the marketing of world music remains a challenge. Few of these acts appear on Jay Leno. To even come close to filling the Hollywood Bowl, which has a capacity of 18,000, is no easy feat. This requires a delicate balancing act between a known headliner—Sergio Mendes, for example—and a lesser-known opening act. This is the art Schnabel practices each summer for his series.

Sometimes I think about all the people who have immigrated to the United States over the years, and about all their children who traveled to California to make their homes here. I think of Los Angeles, where we travel on the freeways and drive around in a constant stream of traffic—and the varieties of music that are the soundtrack to our lives.

In Hollywood, one of the memorable landmarks is The Crossroads of the World, on Sunset Boulevard. Thanks to Schnabel and Shah-Rais among others, Los Angeles is becoming the crossroads of world music.

March 16, 2006

GROSSMAN REVEALED

The recent publication of *A Writer at War: Vasily Grossman With the Red Army, 1941-1945* (Pantheon) brings attention to a writer who deserves to be better known and whose personal story illuminates the tragic dimension of Russian Jewry during the Communist era.

Grossman (1905-1964) was a journalist as well as the author of short stories and novels, most notably *Life and Fate,* which is to be reissued this spring by New York Review Books Classics. His reporting during World War II was the great crucible in which he forged himself as a person and as a writer, and it was what made him famous. What he witnessed during the war also fueled his great disappointment with Soviet society during the second half of his life.

Grossman was raised in Berdichev, once considered "the most Jewish city in Ukraine"—half its population of 60,000 were Jewish. Grossman, however, was fully assimilated and never practiced Judaism. He and his family embraced the Russian revolution enthusiastically, hoping that communism would mean an end to the pogroms and racial discrimination that had rained on Jews until then. And it did, at first.

Thanks to the Soviet regime, Grossman attended high school, was sent to Moscow University where he earned a degree in chemistry in 1929 and was able to find work as a scientist. For all this he was grateful, as it would have been almost impossible under the czarist regime. But more important to Grossman, he was able to become a writer—and he was appreciative of the opportunities the state provided.

His stories helped him gain admittance to the Soviet Writer's Union. As a successful writer, the state treated him well: He was paid handsomely, had good housing (an apartment in the center of Moscow) and was invited (and allowed) to take his family on vacation to a dacha on the Black Sea.

When war broke out with Germany in 1941, Grossman, a patriot, volunteered for service. He was rejected as too old and not physically fit. Undeterred, Grossman went to the offices of Krasnaya Zvezda (Red Star), the official Red Army newspaper and asked to be sent to the front.

There is a long tradition of writers going to war. On the American side, certainly Stephen Crane, Ernest Hemingway and Norman Mailer come to mind. On the Soviet side, Tolstoy's *War and Peace* looms large (although Tolstoy himself did not experience the Napoleonic assault on Moscow); and before Grossman, there was Isaac Babel who rode with the Cossacks.

Grossman spent 1,000 days covering the war, more than any other Soviet reporter. He covered the original German advance though Ukraine, the battle in the South and he was there for the battle of Stalingrad.

He was respected by infantry and generals alike for his courage under fire. His accounts were read by the general public and the troops and were universally admired for delivering what Grossman called, "the ruthless truth of war."

Through his reporting, one experiences how Russia, unprepared for war, endured enormous casualties to stop the German advance, in the process transforming itself into a victorious fighting machine that turned the tide of the combat against the Nazis on the Eastern Front.

A Writer at War, edited and translated by Antony Beevor (a historian of Stalingrad), and Luba Vinogradova is based on Grossman's notebooks. However, while the authors do their best to give context to each comment integrated with excerpts from Grossman's reportage—what is missing is more Grossman. Reading this book just made me want to read the actual accounts.

The battle of Stalingrad transformed Grossman. Just as it changed the course of the war, Grossman believed that moment would redefine the Soviet nation. The soldiers' bravery and their unity were, for Grossman, the socialist dream realized. He believed that what he witnessed during the war, both the good and the bad, would help the Soviet nation become the just, egalitarian society he believed it could be. He was to be deeply disappointed.

Grossman followed the Soviet army as it reclaimed Ukraine, and he was there as it uncovered the crimes of the Nazi regime—the mass murders and the mass graves. He learned that in his hometown of Berdichev, over the course of two days after the Germans arrived, the entire Jewish population of 30,000 men, women and children were marched to a ditch outside town and shot.

"There are no Jews in Ukraine," Grossman wrote. "All is silence. Everything is still. A whole people has been brutally murdered."

In 1944, Grossman was among the first reporters at the Majdanek concentration camp, and then among the first to arrive at the great cemetery of Polish Jewry, Treblinka. Grossman's reporting on the latter, *The Hell of Treblinka,* was read into evidence at the Nuremberg trials. Grossman was with the Soviet troops as they entered Berlin, and he visited Hitler's compound in the Chancellery (and pocketed some stamps and souvenirs from the Fuhrer's office that remained in his desk until the day he died).

The Soviet authorities encouraged Grossman to be part of the Jewish Anti-Fascist Committee, an international organization founded by Albert Einstein, among others, to record the crimes and atrocities committed against Jews by the Nazis and their collaborators. Grossman and Ilya Ehrenberg collected accounts and reports of the murder of Soviet Jews. But once assembled, "The Black Book," as it was called, was suppressed by the Soviet authorities, who now deemed singling out the death of the Jews as too "nationalistic" in accordance with Stalin's decree: "Do not divide the dead" (which meant don't mention that they are Jewish). "The Black Book" would not be published until 1968, after Grossman's death; and only at first in the West, smuggled out of Russia, thanks to Andrei Sakharov and Vladimir Voinovich.

Grossman was bitterly disappointed by the Soviet turn against his account, but his novel of Stalingrad, *For a Just Cause,* nevertheless drew praise. He believed that the message of Stalingrad would help to create a more just society. But Grossman could not have been more wrong. This was the time when Stalin began his purges; his "doctors' trial" signaled the return of state-sponsored anti-Semitism.

Grossman found himself criticized in the pages of Pravda. Even after Stalin's death, which Grossman hoped would signal a new openness, he suffered. The Soviet authorities refused to publish Grossman's epic novel *Life and Fate* which he submitted for review in 1960. He appealed directly to Kruschev, but the authorities told him his novel would only give ammunition to the enemies of the Soviet Union. *Life and Fate* was not published in Grossman's lifetime, either.

Here is the irony of the lives of Soviet Jews: Although many were accomplished and assimilated, nonpracticing and nonobservant with little knowledge or experience of things Jewish, their lives were nonetheless defined by being Jewish.

This was painfully true for members of my own family as well. When World War II broke out in 1939, Tarnopol came under Soviet control. My father's cousin, Meyer Teichholz, lived there (today his name is Mike Sherwood). A teenager at the time, he joined the Komsomol (the youth wing of the Communist Party). When the Germans invaded in 1941 he went into hiding. Liberated by the Russians in 1944, he was sent to work in the Urals. There he was arrested on trumped-up political charges and sent to a gulag. Exonerated in 1947, he was repatriated to Poland and from there was able eventually to travel to Israel and then the United States. His older brother, Fedor, remained trapped in the Soviet Union. Although Fedor was a decorated Soviet War hero and a doctor—people in his town in the Urals, referred to him as "the Jew." When it came time to say Kaddish for his parents, he would lock himself in the hall closet for fear the neighbors would hear him speaking Hebrew and denounce him to the authorities.

Grossman had a secret, too. He always regretted that when war broke out with Germany, he had not traveled back to Berdichev to rescue his mother. By the time, Grossman realized the speed of the German advance, it was too late.

That Grossman could not save his mother who was murdered for being a Jew; that the Soviet state he believed in, and had witnessed in all its glory in Stalingrad, would not let him speak out about the murder of the Jews by the Nazis and their collaborators; that the Stalin would promote state-sponsored anti-Semitism; and that Kruschev who served at Stalingrad would not publish his novel "Life and Fate," all this left Grossman feeling deeply betrayed. In the end, he realized whom he was and what he had to do.

Just before Vasily Grossman died of stomach cancer in 1964, he made a last request: that his coffin not be put on display in the Writer's Union building. He also didn't want to be buried in a Writer's Union plot, preferring to be buried in Moscow's Jewish cemetery. After he died, Grossman's wife requested that he be buried among Russia's elite in Moscow's Novodevichy Cemetery. Neither request was honored. Grossman lies instead in Troyekurovskoye Cemetery just outside of Moscow, waiting, like his great works, to be rediscovered.

March 30, 2006

VRBA'S FIVE PERCENT

On April 7, 1944, Rudolf Vrba escaped from Auschwitz, one of very few to do so; he died last week at age eighteen, a professor of pharmacology at the University of Vancouver, British Columbia. Vrba once said that he spent ninety-five percent of his life on science and five percent on the Holocaust. It is worth considering the importance of that five percent and the controversy it engendered, which resonates to this day.

Vrba was born Walter Rosenberg in 1924 and grew up in Czechoslovakia. At fifteen, he was barred from attending school because he was Jewish. He became a laborer until he was arrested in 1942 and sent first to Majdanek and then to Auschwitz. He worked for many months in the arrivals area, watching the overfilled human cargo trains pull in and sorting the goods of the soon-to-be-dead. At a later date, he was transferred to Birkenau, where he worked in the quarantine area, registering those whose illnesses prevented them from immediately being murdered. There he could glimpse the gas chambers and came into contact with the sonderkommando, Jewish inmates whose job was to drag the bodies from the gas chambers to the crematoria.

In the quarantine section, Vrba met fellow inmate Alfred Wetzler (also spelled Weczler) who had worked in various areas of Auschwitz-Birkenau, and between them, they had a comprehensive understanding of the camps and their operation. They decided—against all reason, all information and even against the advice of some Jewish leaders in the camp—to escape. They were driven not only to save their own lives but to tell the world what they had seen. Vrba, in particular, was concerned because he had witnessed a new railroad spur being built and had overheard that this was meant for the Jews of Hungary who would soon be coming to Auschwitz to meet their fate.

Vrba and Wetzler escaped by hiding at the perimeter of the camp, where materials were kept for constructing an extension of the grounds. They hid for three days under planks in a woodpile and spread near them tobacco and some gasoline to hide their scent from the guard dogs. After three days, the Germans stopped searching for them. Only then did they emerge and actually make their escape.

Eventually, they crossed from Poland to Slovakia and made contact with leaders of the Jewish resistance, whom they told what they had witnessed. It was shocking—no one had escaped Auschwitz before—and no one had ever described the camp and its operation in such exacting detail.

The Jewish leaders knew that their friends and family members had been transported to the camps in the east—but even they could not grasp a systematic factory of death where plunder and murder were done in an assembly line process. They questioned Vrba and Wetzler each separately to make sure their stories matched and redacted their accounts in Hungarian and German into a thirty-two page account that became known as the Vrba-Wetzler report and as *The Auschwitz Protocols.*

Copies were prepared: One was given to Rabbi Michael Dov-Ber Weissmandel to send to Jewish representatives in Switzlerland, who in turn sent it the United States, where it was brought to President Franklin D. Roosevelt's attention. Another was given to the representative of the pope in Slovakia, who forwarded it to the Vatican. Finally, Vrba insisted that a copy be sent to the Hungarian Jewish leadership to warn them of what the Nazis had planned for them.

The Nazis had invaded Hungary and occupied Budapest on March 19, 1944. Up until then, Budapest's Jews lived in relative safety. However, with Adolf Eichmann now in command, the Nazis immediately began imposing restrictive laws and regulations.

The Hungarian Jewish Rescue and Relief Committee (also called the Waada) was headed by two men, Joel Brand and Rudolf (Rezo) Kastner. Kastner arrived in Bratislava on April 28, 1944, and was given a copy of the Wetzler-Vrba report. And herein the controversy begins.

Once the world knew of Auschwitz, what did it do? What did Roosevelt do? What actions did the pope take? And what of the Hungarian Jews themselves?

The gas chambers at Auschwitz continued to operate until late October 1944—of 800,000 Hungarian Jews, only about 80,000 survived the war—Vrba felt that the world powers did not do enough, and that because the Hungarian Jewish leadership did not inform the entire Hungarian Jewish population of the Nazis' plans, hundreds of thousands of Jewish lives were lost that might have been saved. Vrba titled his memoir, *I Cannot Forgive.*

Why didn't Kastner distribute the Wetzler-Vrba report among the Jewish populace?

Many accounts suggest that the Waada didn't want to "alarm" the population. But there is also another reason given: On April 25, 1944, Eichmann, architect of the Final Solution, summoned Brand to his new offices in the Majestic Hotel in Budapest. After explaining that he was the one responsible for the "aktions" against Jews in Germany, Poland and Czechoslovakia, Eichmann made a shocking declaration: "I am prepared to sell you 1 million Jews."

Recently, I read Brand's account of this meeting and what ensued in *Desperate Mission, Joel Brand's Story*, by Alex Weissberg (Criterion, 1958). It is chilling and mind numbing to imagine being in the room with Eichmann and hearing such a proposal. It is even more heartbreaking to read what followed: Brand was dispatched to get the approval and funds from the Jewish Agency leadership in Constantinople (Istanbul). Although he was expected to return in two weeks, instead Brand was led on a wild goose chase that had him travel to Aleppo in Syria and to Cairo, where he was interrogated by British authorities. Along the way, he met with Jewish leaders Moshe Shertok, David Ben-Gurion and Teddy Kollek.

Months passed. No one helped. No one acted. Instead, the Jewish leaders parachuted "fighters" into Eastern Europe, who were immediately arrested, including Hannah Senesh who was put to death by the Nazis in a Budapest jail cell.

Back in Budapest, Kastner kept the negotiations alive with Eichmann and his surrogates, most notably an SS man named Kurt Becker. Eventually, they succeeded in having a train of some 1,600 Jews sent to Switzerland. Kastner believed, as Brand had, that the war was going to end imminently. They thought they just had to stall a little longer to save Jewish lives.

On July 19, 1944, Hungarian Prime Minister Miklos Horthy stopped the deportations to the camps. However, the Hungarian fascists, the Arrow Cross Party, toppled Horthy and resumed a policy of murdering Jews, which continued unabated until the Russians liberated Budapest in January, 1945.

After the war, Kastner immigrated to Israel, where he worked in a government ministry. When a fellow Hungarian immigrant, Malchiel Greenwalt, attacked Kastner as a Nazi collaborator, Kastner sued for libel. The Kastner trial, as it came to be called, became a trial of Kastner's behavior during the war—whether he deliberately did not inform Hungarian Jewry of the Nazis' plan and let hundreds of thousands die in order to save the 1,600 members of the Kastner train, which included some of his friends and relatives.

He was faulted for having provided an affidavit for Becker at his war crimes trial, saying they had worked together to save Jews. The judge concluded that Kastner had "sold his soul to Satan" in dealing with Eichmann and Becker. Soon after, the Ben-Gurion government fell. American writer and Irgun supporter Ben Hecht wrote a play called "Perfidy," critical of Kastner and those who would negotiate rather than resist.

However, on appeal, the Supreme Court of Israel reversed the verdict, saying Kastner had only done what any person in his situation would have done. But it was too late: Kastner had been assassinated on a Tel Aviv street a few months earlier. His murderer was never found.

Eichmann, for his part, fled to Argentina, where in 1961 he was apprehended by Israeli agents and brought to trial in

Jerusalem. Brand and his wife, Hansi, testified against him. In his testimony, Eichmann implied that he used Kastner to keep order among the Jews during the deportations. Holocaust revisionists have used Eichmann's comments and Vrba's arguments as fodder for the contention that the Jews were complicit in their own murders.

So what are we to think? No one really knows what Eichmann intended. Were his negotiations with the Jewish community a way to distract the Jewish leaders and lull them into submission as he pursued his Final Solution? Would he really have saved 1 million lives if he had received the payment he demanded? Was all this a plan or a ploy by Eichmann—or even Himmler—to create an opening to the Allies after the U.S. invasion at Normandy and the approaching Soviet forces? Was this a way to say, as Becker did at his war crimes trial: "We wanted to save Jews"?

Did Brand and Kastner make tragic judgment calls? Or was Kastner guided purely by self-interest? How can we second guess him? If the Auschwitz protocols had been circulated among the Hungarian Jewish populace, would more have survived? Would people have even believed them as true?

Remember, that since 1939, more than 25,000 Jewish refugees had flooded Hungary, and many had reported on the fate of Polish Jewry, the ghettos and camps there and had established a resistance organization (which reported to Brand and Kastner). If Auschwitz's purpose was not known, certainly the Nazi and Arrow Cross plans for Jewish annihilation were.

What we do know for sure is as follows: Vrba and Wetzler's report did confirm the worst fears of the Jewish leadership. Roosevelt and the pope shortly thereafter did condemn the deportations and Horthy did act to halt the deportations. Kastner did save more than 1,600 Jewish lives. Some sources (and I'm not sure how they calculated this) estimate that as a result of the Vrba-Wetzler report, 100,000 lives were saved.

After the war, Vrba did doctoral and post-doctoral work in Prague. He became a medical researcher in Israel, Britain, the United States and Canada. Wetzler became a journalist and author, writing under the name Jozef Lanik. He died in 1988 in Slovakia.

The questions remain: How do we ponder the imponderable? How do we act? Given what we know of Bosnia, Rwanda, Darfur (and these are just the places whose names have become totems to us), what can we do? What should we do?

Vrba knew he had to tell the world what he had witnessed. The world, for its part, found it hard to listen, but in the end, it could not ignore the facts. Vrba's 5 percent still haunts us to this day.

April 20, 2006

A GRAHAM OF ROCK

Here's a strange coincidence: Both my doctor and my rabbi share the same leisure pursuit: They are passionate about attending rock concerts. U2, The Stones, Bob Dylan, Bruce Springsteen—If they perform, my good doctors of the body and the soul will attend. They both say it's their way of relaxing from the stress of their respective jobs (and let's face it, being in charge of my physical and spiritual well-being is some daunting task).

It's not that I find this coincidence so strange...It's just that doctors used to be into things like collecting kaleidoscopes, sailing, playing golf or squash and bad real estate investments and rabbis—well I'm not sure rabbis had hobbies other than the traditional staying up all night with the students, fleeing Cossacks or marching in civil rights rallies.

Although I associate the relentless pursuit of rock concerts as a student activity, it makes sense that this has become a leisure pursuit of the baby boomer professional class—a Four Seasons version of their student days—featuring the same bands as they saw (or wished they had seen) in their salad days, only now at exorbitant expense (i.e. ticket brokers, sky boxes, all to the tune of hundreds of dollars, and T-shirts that start at $40). Yes, everything old is new again, and like an iPod on shuffle, we are trapped in an endless looped cycle of our cultural references.

As I write this, I am listening to CD a friend gave me of a Grateful Dead concert we attended together in high school. I must confess that it sounds like I am hearing it for the first time—and God knows what it is I heard then.

And, coincidentally, by virtue of a new Web site, www.wolfgangsvault.com, I have been revisiting my wasted youth, much of which was spent at the Fillmore East in New York.

Wolfgang's vault refers to the archives of Bill Graham, the concert promoter, born Wolfgang Grajonca, who ran the Fillmore West beginning in 1966 and the Fillmore East beginning in 1968 until it closed in 1971, and after that produced many, many concerts and tours until his untimely death in 1991 in a helicopter crash. Although musical omnivores Clear Channel purchased Graham's business, they agreed several years ago to sell Graham's archives to Bill Sagan, a Minneapolis businessman who has set up the Wolfgang's vault Web site to stream performances, as well as sell rock memorabilia.

Graham, whom I interviewed in 1986 for Interview Magazine, was born in Berlin in 1931 to Russian Jewish parents. His father died two days after he was born. Graham was the youngest child and the only boy among five sisters. As the situation in Germany got worse for Jews, his mother sent him and the youngest sister, Tolla, on a kindertransport, which placed them in an orphanage in France.

His eldest sister, Rita, had gone to Shanghai; another sister, Evelyn, fled to Budapest, living on false papers. His mother remained in Berlin, only to be arrested by the SS; she died in a train car on the way to Auschwitz. His sister, Esther, was hidden in a convent in Vienna, but when it was no longer safe there she traveled to Budapest, only to be put on the first train to Auschwitz, from which she survived. Sonja, another sister, also escaped to Budapest, hid there, and ended up living in Vienna after the war.

As for Graham, when the orphanage was no longer safe, a Red Cross worker led him, his sister and the other Jewish children out of France on a journey that took them to Madrid. On the way, his sister fell sick, and Graham was persuaded to let her be taken to a hospital, where she died. He continued on to Lisbon and Casablanca before sailing to Dakar, Bermuda and Cuba, finally arriving in New York in late 1941. After being placed in a Jewish foster home in upstate New York and then settling with a family in the Bronx, Graham attended Dewitt High school. At 18, he formally changed his name to Bill Graham and attended City College before being drafted for service in the Korean War.

Graham liked to say he was reborn at thirty-five. He had moved to San Francisco and was moonlighting as the business manager of the San Francisco Mime Troupe. When the troupe was busted for a performance that was deemed too "risqué," Graham staged a benefit concert in a loft with, among others, Allen Ginsberg, the Jefferson Airplane and the Fugs. It was so successful and overcrowded that he staged two more, this time at the Fillmore Auditorium. Graham had found his calling. His first nonbenefit concerts were held at the Fillmore on Feb 4, 5, and 6, 1966, with Jefferson Airplane as the headliners.

Graham opened the Fillmore East on March 8, 1968, with Big Brother and the Holding Company, featuring Janis Joplin, in what had once been a movie palace called the Village Theatre, on Second Avenue and Sixth Street, a few doors down from Ratner's dairy restaurant.

Graham was gruff and combative—he resented being labeled "the businessman." As he told me, he saw himself as part of an alternative culture expressed by the performers he was closest to—Joplin, The Dead, Dylan and The Stones—who, voluntarily or involuntary, the public came to see as leaders. Graham gave birth to the modern rock concert phenomenon and saw himself as the enabler of the counterculture, creating communities through events that ranged from Woodstock to Live Aid.

As the promoter, Graham saw himself as having the last word in a democracy created in the service of the artists and the audience. As a member of that audience, I can honestly say, that I never felt Graham was taking advantage of me (as I do today at so many concerts). He gave good value at the Fillmore East.

Thanks to a wonderful book by Amalie Rothschild, *Live at the Fillmore East: A Photographic Memoir* (Thunder's Mouth Press, 1999, co-authored with Ruth Ellen Gruber), a chronicle more evocative than any dosed Madeleine, I was able to revisit the marquee, the ticket booth, the stage, the balcony, the view from the orchestra, the artists, the light show—all the details of a run-down wonderland locked faraway in the recesses of my mind, including the final image of the Fillmore East marquee with Graham's parting words to his audience, "Thank you and farewell."

Even more memory challenging, Rothschild included a list of every concert performed at the Fillmore East. Looking it over was pretty shocking. I remember sitting in the balcony the first time the Who performed *Tommy* in America—and the incredible light show the Fillmore had organized around it. I have an indelible memory of the Grateful Dead's Pigpen playing stage right on the keyboards and sending flares up into the air as he was playing. Santana, Mountain—I know I saw them at the Fillmore—but others—such as Jeff Beck, Poco, Hot Tuna, Traffic, Johnny Winter—did I see them at the Fillmore or somewhere else? I'm no longer sure.

Here's another thing I learned. As I looked at the dates of the shows that I know I attended—I realized that I went to several before I had turned fourteen. Talk about being in a den of iniquity. You might ask: what were my parents thinking?

But it now comes back to me. During the summer of my 13th year, my family went on a European vacation (our first). In Vienna, we visited with Sonja Szobel, who my father had helped escape from a prison in Budapest during the war. She told my father that her brother had just opened up a concert hall in New York, the Fillmore East. My father figured that if her brother was running it, I could go there on my own. It would be fine.

And it was.

May 4, 2006

A PEACE OF MUSIC

How does an idea come to life? How is it that someone has an idea—an idea that he or she believes will help change the world—and it actually takes flight? I'm not sure anyone really knows how that process occurs, only that it does.

Just ask Zade.

Zade Dirani, twenty-six, is a composer and musician who created the International Musicians Assembly, an internationally diverse group of musicians and future leaders from conflict-ridden countries who have recently embarked on their "Roads to You: Celebration of One World" tour.

The LA stopover kicks off at the Museum of Tolerance on May 31 (co-sponsored by The Jewish Journal). It's followed by a members-only performance at Sinai Temple on June 2, as part of the synagogue's 100th anniversary (see story on page 16); and a concert at UCLA's Royce Hall on June 6, where the International Children's Peace Choir from Long Beach will join in.

The tour is the manifestation of Zade's vision of musicians as world leaders making connections through music and culture.

Naiive? Unrealistic? Zade doesn't think so—and he has the life story to back that belief.

Zade was born and raised in Amman, Jordan. His architect father had ambitions for him to follow in his footsteps, but early on Zade showed musical promise (he started composing at thirteen) and was accepted at Jordan's National Music Conservatory. At eighteen, he received a scholarship to study at the Berklee School of Music in Boston.

For the next few years, Zade traveled back and forth between the two. He appeared with the National Symphony of Jordan, where he first performed for Queen Noor, the American-born wife of the late King Hussein. In the United States, Zade organized a series of "house concerts" performing his piano compositions in peoples' homes.

On September 11, 2001, Zade was scheduled to give a concert in Maine at an American friend's home. When news of the attacks spread, the concert was postponed.

"After 9/11," Zade said, "I felt a tremendous responsibility."

As a Muslim and an Arab, playing in the homes of American families, he wanted to bring a message that culture could unite people. At the same time, he also wanted to send a message to his fellow Muslims and Arabs that, "You can be proud of your culture."

Zade threw himself into performing, grass-roots-style, in churches, synagogues and people's homes all over the country, playing as many as 200 concerts in a year. He discovered that through music, he made a personal connection with an audience. Like a latter-day Bob Hope, this performer embraced the role of ambassador.

Zade's performances had another unexpected side effect—he developed a wide-ranging fan base. Zade's first recordings, self-released are now turning up on Billboard charts. His new album *Beautiful World* released on May 16 features compositions redolent of Middle Eastern rhythms as well as classical piano compositions. He has become one of Jordan's best-known artists, performing not only for King Abdullah and Queen Reina, but such dignitaries as Queen Elizabeth II, Nelson Mandela and the Dalai Lama. Like Madonna, Zade has ascended to one-name recognition.

However, Zade wanted to do more. Working alone, he was delivering, in essence, a monologue—about culture and heritage and the connections people can make between the two. What he wanted was a dialogue.

Zade sought out other musicians from conflict-ridden countries or regions—talented musicians who also had leadership qualities and were interested in developing conflict-resolution skills.

He also quickly found three sponsors. His alma mater, The Berklee College of Music, agreed to be an educational partner; the Barakat Foundation, which supports culture and cultural exchanges and operates under the sponsorship of Queen Noor, signed on as philanthropic partner; and Seeds of Peace, an organization that brings together young Israelis and Palestinians, helps with conflict-resolution programs and leadership training.

The Jordanian embassy contacted other embassies to suggest applicants; Berklee helped identify candidates as well. Over a period of many months, Zade assembled a troupe of thirty-five musicians, ages eighteen to thirty, from eighteen countries, including Israel, Iran, Korea, China and Mexico.

Under the name The International Musicians Assembly, they perform Zade's compositions. The musicians also appear as trios, quartets and septets, frequently performing their own compositions. Particularly popular is the Abrahamic Trio, a constellation that featured Ali Bekrahdi, a Muslim from Iran, on santur (Persian hammer dulcimer); Perla Martinez, a Christian from Mexico on violin; and Jake Hertzog, a Jew from Michigan, on electric guitar. On any given day, eight different ensembles hold musical workshops and speak at schools and before other audiences about themselves, their countries and their music.

Zade has a five-year strategy. He hopes this group spawns many others, so that on any given night, somewhere in the world, a group of musicians/leaders are performing and opening people's hearts.

He already has inspired numerous others to get involved, including Dr. Nur Amersi, the honorary director of the International Musicians Assembly. The Santa Monica-based Amersi practiced veterinary medicine for a decade before committing herself to philanthropy, as the Western U.S. representative of the Aga Khan's institute of Ismali Studies.

"In these troubled times," Amersi said, "musical initiatives become tools that promote human and cultural pluralism—thereby becoming an effective force of stability."

Music is no certain path to peace (i.e. consider the East Coast-West Coast rap wars), but Zade sees culture as a powerful positive force. Zade's mission calls to mind Isaac Bashevis Singer's saying that "the good life is not passive existence where you live and let live. It is one of involvement where you live and help live."

Zade, four years shy of age thirty, already knows that.

May 18, 2006

GREAT SCOTT

Scott Steindorff is a happy man. A successful movie and TV producer, his NBC series, *Las Vegas,* just got picked up for another season; he won an Golden Globe for the HBO miniseries, *Empire Falls,* starring Paul Newman, and produced the feature film of Philip Roth's *The Human Stain* with Anthony Hopkins and Nicole Kidman. Upcoming on Steindorff's slate are adaptations of Gabriel Garcia Marquez's *Love in the Time of Cholera,* TC Boyle's *The Tortilla Curtain,* Michael Connolly's *The Lincoln Lawyer, Penelope* starring Reese Witherspoon and remakes of the classic films *Ikiru* and *Rififi.* All this and he's only been in the film business six years.

Very few people arrive in Hollywood already in their 40s and succeed in becoming producers. Even among those who do manage to get a film made (a miracle in itself), one-hit wonders abound and legions have given up after a just few seasons in the sun. To succeed in both TV and film is rare—rarer still for a relative newcomer.

So let's pay attention to the story of Scott Steindorff.

Steindorff was born in a small town in Minnesota. When he was young, his family moved to Arizona, where his father was involved in real estate. As a young man, he was passionate about theater, skiing (he made the U.S. Olympic team) and books.

"I grew up reading books," Steindorff told me recently. "We didn't watch TV."

Steindorff attended Arizona State, pursuing a dual major in theater and business. He wanted to go to Hollywood to act in movies, but his father wanted him to go into business.

Given what I know of Jewish fathers and sons, I sometimes wonder if what preceded Abraham taking his son to be sacrificed was Isaac telling him he wanted to be an artist rather than go into business. Many a child's artistic career has been sacrificed on the mount by a parent's plea.

So no surprise: Steindorff went into the family real estate business and spent the next two decades developing land and shopping centers.

Then came the 1990s real estate slump. Steindorff moved to California hoping to write or act in movies (he did manage to appear in some skiing movies). To keep himself financially afloat he did real estate consulting, which brought him to Las Vegas. Working as a consultant to the Forum Shops at Caesar's Palace—which became an attraction unto themselves—led to his being hired by Caesar's as an entertainment consultant.

When Tommy Tune took over the MGM Grand's show *EFX*, Steindorff wrote the new version himself—which was a big hit. This taste of show business success led to Steindorff's "now or never" moment.

Six years ago, at forty, he made the decision "to pursue the entertainment business full blast." But unlike his earlier forays into Hollywood as a potential actor or writer, this time he took a different approach—as a producer.

Which is not as easy as it sounds.

Although every year brings, like the swallows to Capistrano, a flock of self-anointed movie producers to Los Angeles, Hollywood is actually a small club that doesn't really like outsiders. The gatekeepers and decision makers are generally people who've been working in the industry their entire professional lives, for or with those corporate entities we call "the studios."

Generally, to break in you have to have something the studios want—access to a star, or exclusive control of a best-selling or newsworthy book or story. Or money.

Hollywood has always been happy to greet new money. However, many wealthy people have had their wallets lightened by virtue of developing projects that didn't get made; or, worse yet, ones that got made and were just as quickly forgotten. But as happy as Hollywood is to take new money, they are slower to award any respect to those they dismiss as merely "money people." (And that, in my opinion, is what the whole Bob Yari/ *Crash* suit is really all about.)

So how has Steindorff achieved his success? To get Hollywood's attention he realized that, yes, he would need a bag of money. But more important would be how he chose to spend it.

Although many people deride Las Vegas as a cultural backwater, Steindorff had found himself surrounded by good friends who cared deeply about books and movies. He garnered a group of Las Vegas investors (including Danny Greenspun, son of the legendary Las Vegas publisher Hank Greenspun), and then with their backing he started to buy film rights to pedigreed popular literary books.

Steindorff's gamble was that he would be judged not by his money (or not only by his money) but by his taste. And rather than just handing off the money to third parties, Steindorff and his company, Stone Village Entertainment, used their own money to acquire properties—much like a real estate deal—enabling Steindorff to maintain involvement in the projects and keep his position as a producer.

So, on the one hand, he is a businessman: "I'm an entrepreneur. But I take less of a risk when I go after the best." (Think of blue-chip properties.) Hence his portfolio contains Nobel, Pulitzer and National Book Award winners. This business approach is the key to his art.

Today, although Steindorff admits that he spent many years resenting that he followed his father's wishes, he feels his business background served him well.

Perhaps on that day long ago when Abraham stood poised above his son, Isaac, the Good Lord whispered in his ear, "Not to worry: I will create a business out of art for your son and his children and their children to pursue." Perhaps Isaac wondered what such an enterprise could be—and God said "I'll show you—I'll call it Show Business."

And it came to be that both father and son were pleased. Just ask Scott Steindorff.

Among the properties that Steindorff recently acquired is A.M. Homes' *This Book Will Save Your Life.* Although it received a particularly unkind review from The New York Times, the novel had a particular resonance for Steindorff, a divorced father of three, a man who finally got to live his dream. Homes' book is about a man who decides to change his life. Steindorff did that, and he can't believe his good fortune.

"I love my life," Steindorff says. Hanging out with Paul Newman; having dinner with Philip Roth; on the set with Reese Witherspoon. Sounds good.

Which reminds me of a quote from George Eliot (the pen name of Mary Ann Evans), who said, "It is never too late to become what you might have been."

June 1, 2006

SUMMER SCHOOL WITH SCHIMMEL

Paul Schimmel, the Museum of Contemporary Art's (MOCA) chief curator, wants us to spend our summer looking back—fifty or so years to around the time of his birth, and to the city where he grew up, New York, to focus on the remarkable work of a young, poor and not-yet-famous Robert Rauschenberg, who was gathering junk and detritus from his life (clothes, family photos, fabric) and incorporating them into paintings that then became three-dimensional constructs, which Rauschenberg called *Combines.*

Although the *Combines* are well-known to art lovers, and certainly Rauschenberg's *Monogram* (or "That work with the stuffed goat," as most people know it) has achieved iconic status, no previous show has ever focused exclusively on the *Combines.*

Schimmel believes that the *Combines* are among the most important and influential works of the second half of the twentieth century—that they operate not only as a bridge between the abstract expressionists and the pop artists, but also contain the seeds of many art movements that followed. He also argues that the *Combines* are even more culturally relevant today in the age of sampling and in a culture that cannibalizes itself at an unprecedented rate.

Schimmel believes that this exhibition of Rauschenberg's work, *"Robert Rauschenberg: Combines,"* which he organized for MOCA and which had its first showing last winter at the Metropolitan Museum of Art in New York, will have a major influence on other artists' work over the next ten to fifteen years. And this kind of thinking—the long-view historical perspective, the focus on artists, the pop cultural references and this sort of grandiose pronouncement (which could very well be dead on)—is all typical of Schimmel.

Schimmel is toastmaster and host at the hippest party in town, the LA contemporary art scene. He has been chief curator at MOCA since 1990, and during his tenure the contemporary art world and the LA art scene have exploded—never have so many collectors been so globally active in the acquisition of recently made art. Never have so many Los Angeles-based artists been so well regarded by the art establishment. MOCA has garnered serious consideration, in part, by virtue of Schimmel's major exhibitions, which have tried to give both historical context to contemporary work as well as to focus on the output of many individual artists.

So how did Paul Schimmel get to be Paul Schimmel? Turns out, strange as it may seem, that he has always been Paul Schimmel.

"Even in high school," Schimmel recalled recently, "I wanted to be a curator."

He credits the influence of his Manhattan private school art teacher, Betty Tompkins, an artist he describes as a "photo-realist with a strong feminist bent" and whose work has recently been receiving renewed attention. He also points to his high school English teacher, Paul Schwager, who suggested that

Schimmel do his eleventh-grade project on Gertrude Stein. For that project, Schimmel began spending time at the library of the Museum of Modern Art (MOMA), where the librarian, impressed that a fifteen-year-old was so passionate about art, introduced him to some of the associate curators. They, in turn, learning that his project was on Stein, took him to see original works in the museum's collection that, by coincidence, they just happened to be in the process of organizing for a landmark show on the Stein and Cone collections. "I felt this was the coolest," Schimmel said.

As a teenager, Schimmel would walk friends through MOMA and the Met.

"I had these different tours that I would do," he said. "I always felt museums were an extension of my house."

He realized that he did not need to own the artworks to feel that they were his own: "By looking at something, spending time with it, talking about it, it became my work."

Or, more to the point, Schimmel realized that looking and talking about artworks could become his life's work.

"In some ways," Schimmel now says, "nothing has changed since then. To this day, [this approach] continues to inform what I do as a curator."

He attended Syracuse University, where he was allowed to take some of the graduate-level museum studies program courses, and did an internship at the Contemporary Arts Museum (CAM) in Houston. Upon graduation, he joined the curatorial staff of CAM, spending several years in Texas before returning to New York to the Institute of Fine Arts, an art history program at New York University, to work toward a master's degree. After leaving NYU in 1981, he was offered a job as a curator at the Newport Harbor Art Museum (which is now the Orange County Museum of Art).

Schimmel admitted that the first day he arrived in Orange County from New York "was a shock." At first he felt "like I was in a satellite—removed."

Yet he found that the expectations of what he could accomplish there were such that when he exhibited edgy and ground-breaking contemporary Los Angeles artists like Mike Kelly, Chris Burden or Charlie Ray, the reaction was: "How did you do that in Newport?"

From the start, Schimmel realized that "you need to engage a younger audience." What he also learned is that if you do a show and get people to write about it, audiences will come, and you get a following. Equally important, you can have a big success with modest numbers. As long as the museum leaders feel the museum is making a contribution to its community, you have the support of the museum. In the just under a decade that he was at the Newport Harbor museum, Schimmel organized a series of major exhibitions including ones on emerging California artists; a reassessment of figurative art from the 1950s, an Edvard Munch show that was hugely successful and a local artists' biennial.

Then, in 1990, Schimmel was offered the MOCA post.

"It was a surprise," he said. "It's not that likely for a major institution of international stature to look so locally."

But Schimmel had the support of a few museum trustees, including the respected collector Marcia Weisman, who liked him for his commitment not only to the California and LA art scene, but for his wide-ranging historical approach to shows.

Schimmel has now been at MOCA for sixteen years, an unusually stable career in a world where art institutions and curators regularly engage in musical chairs.

In many ways he has been at the right place at the right time. He presides over a significant collection of contemporary art at a moment when, as Schimmel put it, "the role of contemporary art has become more central, more visible, more financially significant than anyone can imagine."

In the 1960s, contemporary art was a "very small, highly rarified world." Although there was an explosion of artists and collectors in the 1980s, museums of modern art were uncomfortable with contemporary art. Today the scene is completely different.

"The growth of contemporary art museums in the post-war period in this country was a direct result of the larger more encyclopedic museums keeping two things out," Schimmel said: "Contemporary art and Jews."

"So if you look at the Museum of Contemporary Art in Chicago and the Institute of Contemporary Art in Boston, and the number of contemporary art museums in Los Angeles, younger Jewish collections were at the root." Schimmel defines these collectors as creating a counter culture—meaning a culture counter to the mainstream old master collections. On an international level, the most famous exemplar is Charles Saatchi, an Iraqi-born Jew who made his fortune in advertising and who, despite having advised Margaret Thatcher's Conservative Party on its successful election campaign, is an outsider to the English establishment, and who has had an enormous impact on the contemporary art scene.

In Los Angeles, a similar phenomenon led to the formation of MOCA. Although for most of the twentieth century the Los

Angeles County Museum of Art (LACMA), founded in 1910, was the pre-eminent repository for modern art in Los Angeles, the now-defunct Pasadena Art Museum was once thought to be the place for contemporary art (particularly under Walter Hopps). However, the Pasadena museum foundered financially, and in 1974 Norton Simon took it over and transformed it into his eponymous showcase of impressionist, old master, and Asian art.

In 1979, seeking a home in Los Angeles for contemporary art, Norton Simon's sister, Marcia Weisman, along with her husband Frederick Weisman (they later divorced) and other major contemporary art collectors such as Phil and Beatrice Gersh, Lenore Greenberg, Max Palevsky and Eli Broad, broke away from LACMA, founding MOCA in 1983, after Mayor Tom Bradley suggested creating a museum of contemporary art as part of California Plaza, a downtown Los Angeles hotel and office development. While they awaited construction of the Arata Isozaki building (which opened in 1986), MOCA's first home became a former police garage in Little Tokyo, renovated by Frank Gehry.

The Temporary Contemporary (TC) was always a place where expectations were different—it didn't have the imprimatur of a "museum." But it also afforded the opportunity to exhibit work that didn't fit in the normal confines of traditional museum galleries. This freewheeling openness proved liberating for the curators, the artists, and for the audiences. At the TC you could expect to see avant-garde work, and you were free to hate it, ridicule it or even enjoy it.

The TC proved so popular that it turned out to defy its "temporary" name; it was expanded to include an additional exhibition space, and in 1996 David Geffen contributed $5 million to renovate the space—which resulted in it being renamed the Geffen Contemporary. The space housed the recent successful *Ecstacy: In and About Altered States* show, curated by Schimmel, which is now closed for renovation but will reopen in September.

Schimmel sees the Geffen space as keeping alive the connection between the "studio and the factory." If the Arata Isozaki building is the heart of MOCA, Schimmel said, then the Geffen Contemporary remains "the soul of MOCA."

Was necessity the mother of invention, or was MOCA prescient? In recent years, a number of major art institutions, most notably the Tate in London, have felt a need to renovate industrial space to showcase contemporary work. Could one be so bold as to say they owe a debt to MOCA?

Schimmel feels that one of the reasons that Los Angeles has become home to so many contemporary artists is CalArts—a school that is itself very much artist-led (a case he made persuasively with the exhibition *Public Offerings*). Similarly, Schimmel feels that what distinguishes MOCA as an institution is the involvement of artists, such as the late Sam Francis and the always innovative Robert Irwin as early trustees, as well as architect Frank Gehry, who was once a board member and is still an active supporter.

In some ways, Schimmel said, artists are the audience that matters most to the museum's growth and future.

"Who is our audience?" Schimmel asks. " Tourists? Collectors? Our audience is the artists themselves."

This is a variation on the lesson Schimmel learned in Newport. Put together shows that matter—shows that you are willing to stake your reputation on, shows that artists find interesting and people will write about—and the audience will follow.

"This is not the movie business," Schimmel said, "we don't need millions...We had close to 100,000 visitors for the 'Ecstasy' show, and that's huge by museum standards."

Over the last sixteen years at MOCA, Schimmel has curated numerous thought-provoking shows, including *Helter Skelter: LA Art in the 1990s* (1992), *Hand-painted Pop: American Art in Transition, 1955-62* (1992), *Out of Actions: Between Performance and the Object, 1949-1979* (1998), *Public Offerings* (2001) and *Ecstasy,* as well as solo shows of artists including Sigmar Polke, Robert Gober and Charles Ray.

"I am always mixing historical and contemporary shows." Schimmel said.

Postmodernism has often been critiqued for inserting us into a world without context, into a PC world in which art history is no longer relevant—into a world where the references are only inside jokes or appropriations from other work. Yet Schimmel stands at odds with this point of view.

"I still believe there is a history of art," Schimmel said. "There's a story to be told, and exhibitions that don't attempt to define that history have lost a huge opportunity."

To some extent, MOCA and Paul Schimmel's success lie in seizing that opportunity. Many contemporary art museums have become institutions saddled with demands—large boards, large bureaucracies, the desire for huge shows and large attendance. As a result, increasingly we have witnessed more and more "mega shows" or career retrospectives but fewer historical, conceptual shows. Fewer shows that challenge us to see an artist or an era in a new light.

"MOCA is one of the few museums that consistently takes on large-scale thematic exhibitions." Schimmel said.

He believes MOCA, in this way, is living up to the standard set by the Museum of Modern Art (MOMA) in New York in his teenage years.

"MOCA has done more to embrace and further the legacy of complex theoretical thematic exhibitions than MOMA has done over the last fifteen years," Schimmel said.

Today, MOMA, in the wake of its successful renovation, is an encyclopedia of modern art come to life—the number of major recognizable masterworks in its collection is mind boggling. It is almost overwhelming. One can't fault MOMA for the wealth of its collection. But one can still pine, as Schimmel does, for the clarity that the MOMA of Schimmel's high-school years afforded.

Like Schimmel, I spent a great deal of time at New York's Museum of Modern Art during my high school years (When Schimmel was looking in the basement at their collection, I was probably sitting in the garden staring at Rodin's statue of Balzac and at Picasso's goat). MOMA's then-curator William Rubin had created a museum where one room followed the next, the artworks were all at eye level, accessible. You didn't need an audio tour: the works in each room made the argument that this follows this—allowing the connections to be made in your head.

Rubin taught at NYU when Schimmel was a graduate student—but my guess is it is more the museum than the man that influenced him. When you visit the Combines at MOCA, you are seeing an exhibition that could have been shown at Rubin's MOMA.

I was reminded of this when visiting Schimmel's stunning installation of Rauschenberg's work. The groupings are done in a way that states the importance of each work but allows the viewer space to interact with the art. There is a flow, an art historical progression that allows you to make the connections between abstract expressionism—the messiness, the found objects (while rejecting its emotional quality)—and the coolness of pop art to follow, with its similar interest in newspaper comics and the everyday. At the same time, there is bridge between the work Rauschenberg did before, the red paintings, and what would follow. Finally, the show allows us to consider the importance of the Combines unto themselves, as presaging the work of a wide variety of contemporary artists—from John Baldessari to Robert Gober, just to name a few—and as being uniquely relevant to today (some of the Combines look like they could have been made last week, not fifty years ago).

The Combines show would be reason enough to visit MOCA this summer, but as long as we are there, Schimmel has a few more tours he wants to take us on.

There is a twenty-year survey of the work of Lorna Simpson, an artist whose photographs and video installations, combining images and text, challenge us to consider issues of narrative and gender; as well as a small show titled *After Cézanne,* which is an exquisite selection of works from MOCA's collection that features artists such as Alberto Giacometti, Roy Lichtenstein, Diane Arbus and Arshile Gorky all in conversation with each other—pondering the twentieth century by referencing Cézanne—just as the Combines nearby engage in a dialogue about art in the second half of the twentieth century and into the twenty-first.

So this summer, Paul Schimmel is sending us all back to the future. Summer school is in session at MOCA. Schimmel wants to inspire artists and make them see Rauschenberg's work and their own in a new light. To the collectors and connoisseurs of contemporary art, he wants to reveal the context from which to regard the works that came before and those that will follow. Finally, for the general public he has a special offer: He want us to make these remarkable art works that most of us can never afford our own.

Very, very Paul Schimmel.

June 15, 2006

A LITTLE RESPECT FOR JEWISH JOURNALISM

Jewish journalism is a much-maligned enterprise—it cries out like the late Rodney Dangerfield for respect.

No one really admits to reading a Jewish newspaper. "It comes to my home," is what most people tell me. Or they claim to read it only when they can't get their hands on anything else. "I was at the deli—they have it there." I hear that a lot.

People who seem to actually like what I write are always telling me they wish it were published somewhere else. Somewhere better—i.e., more prestigious, with a larger circulation or certainly a less parochial one...somewhere less, in a word, Jewish.

"It's really good," I'm told as if that would disqualify my work for publication in a Jewish publication.

I won't say that I haven't, on occasion, shared these thoughts about other Jewish papers or Jewish journalism or even about my own ambitions for my writing. But when I do—and particularly on the occasion of The Jewish Journal of Los Angeles' twentieth anniversary—I call to mind the longer view and recall the great history, tradition and noble cause of Jewish journalism.

I'm not sure who qualifies as the first Jewish journalists. It may have been the biblical Caleb and Joshua, who reported on the land of Canaan and brought back the headline: "Flowing With Milk and Honey; Land of Plenty."

Or perhaps it was Josephus (37 C.E.-100 C.E.) who chronicled *The Jewish Wars,* his firsthand account of the Roman conquest of what is today Israel.

Jewish tradition is marked by rendering the oral tradition in print and recording the stories of the patriarchs and matriarchs, the accounts of the prophets, the tales of Kings David and Solomon and the tales of the rabbis. One can argue that the Jewish embrace of the responsibility to bear witness and pass along the stories from generation to generation is the cornerstone for a calling in journalism.

Regardless of the cause or the inspiration, by the late 19th century, Jewish journalism was flourishing, as were Jews who were journalists—some of whom would forever shape the course of journalism and the course of world events.

To give but one notable example: In 1894, among those covering the Paris trial of Capt. Alfred Dreyfus was Theodor Herzl, an Austro-Hungarian journalist. Witnessing the French crowds screaming "Death to the Jews!" profoundly impacted him. Two years later in 1896, Herzl wrote T*he Jewish State,* the rallying cry for Zionism and the establishment of a Jewish homeland. Although he didn't work for a Jewish publication, Herzl entered history when his reporting focused on Jewish matters. Herzl did not live to see the creation of the State of Israel, a mere fifty-two years later, but in recognition of his role in the founding of the state, and as per his wishes, he is buried there today.

In the United States, America's first Jewish newspaper, *The Occident* and *American Jewish Advocate,* was published in 1843 by Philadelphia's Isaac Leeser. More than a decade later in 1854, Rabbi Isaac Mayer Wise of Cincinnati, leader of the Reform movement, founded *The Israelite,* a weekly that proclaimed itself "devoted to the Religion, History and Literature of the Israelites."

Wise, himself an immigrant from Bohemia, was one of the most important Jewish figures of the post-Civil War era. *The Israelite* (later *The American Israelite*) was devoted to helping its readers become, as Wise once wrote, "Americans through and through." However, Wise's greatest contribution to American Journalism may not be The Israelite but rather his daughter, Iphigene "Effie" Wise, who married German Jewish immigrant Adolph Ochs in 1884.

In 1896, Ochs purchased *The New York Times* and set about making it the national newspaper of record. His descendants continue to steer *The Times* to this day.

Around the same time, the Hungarian-born Joseph Pulitzer, who had worked as a journalist for a German-language newspaper, acquired the St. Louis Post, later merging it with the St. Louis Dispatch. Pulitzer continued to acquire newspapers and became famous for sensationalist stories—or "yellow journalism." In spite of that—or maybe because of it—he endowed the Pulitzer Prizes in Journalism at Columbia University.

English was only one of several possible languages for Jewish journalism in the United States. There was also a prevalence of German and Russian. The beginning of the twentieth century saw a flood of Jewish immigration to the United States, bringing in a vast and engaged audience for Jewish papers in many languages, most notably Yiddish.

For many of its readers, there was a special quality to the Yiddish press that is missing from today's Jewish journalism.

Eddie Portnoy, a historian of Yiddish popular culture, said it this way: "The Yiddish press was a private conversation."

It was by Jews for Jews, without concern about what the non-Jewish population might think.

"I think this press was the most important element in modernizing both immigrant Jews, as well as Jews in Eastern Europe." Portnoy told me. "It opened up a literal universe of new people, places, names and concepts. It also served as the birthplace for modern Yiddish literature. And in Russia, this was under the extreme duress of czarist oppression, which permitted only one Yiddish weekly from 1862 to 1889 for a population of nearly 5 million Jews, ninety-seven percent of whom used Yiddish as their mother tongue."

Although many still know the work of literary figures who appeared in the Yiddish press, such as Isaac Bashevis Singer and his older brother, I.J. Singer, lost to time are the many great reporters of the day, who not only covered news but also sports and crime, such as Schlomye Feinkind, whom Portnoy dubbed "the king of the Warsaw crime reporters."

Perhaps the most important American Jewish paper of that era was the Yiddish-language Forverts (Forward), which began as a daily on April 22, 1897, in New York. Founding editor Abraham Cahan, a Russian immigrant, also authored the famous "Bintel Brief" column, giving advice to immigrants. At one point in the first decades of the twentieth century, there were five Yiddish dailies competing for New York's readers, with The Forverts' circulation reaching 275,000.

The Forverts' Yiddish readership declined during the 20th century to the point where by the late 1980s, it had become a weekly. However, in 1990 an English-language independent, weekly publication, *The Forward,* was launched under the editorial leadership of Seth Lipsky. Lipsky has since become editor of the revived *New York Sun*, a paper that a century before had attacked Pulitzer for losing touch with his Jewish ethics.

Among the Jewish publications that furthered the idea of a private conversation were those directed specifically at women. Rabbi Wise's nineteenth-century Israelite published a women's supplement called Devorah. Along with *The American Jewess* (1895-99), these pioneering publications became the catalyst for a growing activism among Jewish women—whose voice would be furthered in such publications as Hadassah and Lilith.

Jewish journalism in the twenty-first century continues to thrive at more than 100 publications nationwide. There are more religious publications than ever before and more sacrilegious ones, as well. There are *American Jewish* newspapers devoted to Israeli and Persian immigrants and others aimed at a new generation of Russians, and there are also new Yiddish publications. In Europe, there is a resurgence of Jewish publications in Hebrew, Russian, German, Yiddish and Hungarian.

Which brings me back to my original point: Don't Jewish newspapers deserve a little more respect?

The Jewish Journal of Los Angeles is celebrating its twentieth anniversary. Personally, I think it's a thought-filled, well-written, well-edited publication that often trumps other LA papers on political, local and arts coverage. But more important, as far as I'm concerned, is that it's a place that I, as a writer and as a reader, can call home.

So go ahead: Read a Jewish paper. And if you enjoy it, tell others. At first, they may be reluctant to admit it, but you may find that they are not only subscribers, they actually read *The*

Journal, as well.

June 29, 2006

LIFE VS. DEATH

In college, I wrote the same literature essay over and over again. Regardless of the novel, its plot or its country of origin, I found that I could always work up four pages on the subject of "Life vs. Death."

My ideas on this subject were not particularly original. In a high school English class, some intellectually precocious seniors had made impassioned references to Norman O. Brown's *Life Against Death* and Freud's discussion of the life force vs. the death force—and to my morbid teenage brain, these ideas stuck. Although it would be years before I would actually read either author, I now had a critical prism by which to analyze literature. It turned out there was no shorter way to a professor's approbation than a mention of liebestot.

I bring this up not only because I find myself again with 1,000 words to write, not only because babies are still being born and people keep dying with alarming regularity, but because the struggle between the forces of life and death came to mind as I read several recent novels.

Phillip Roth's *Everyman,* (Houghton Mifflin) is a short, and in some respects, slight work. Clocking in at around 200 pages, it recounts the life of one man through his medical history. As an organizing principle, this one's as valid as any, even if in this instance, it doesn't necessarily yield the most compelling, multidimensional portrait.

But let me give Roth his due: There are scenes in *Everyman* that continue to haunt me, simple descriptions of mundane events—such as the experience of being wheeled into an operation or of attending a Jewish funeral and hearing the sound of freshly dug earth upon the coffin—that made me experience them anew and deeply in ways that only underline Roth's mastery as a wordsmith and novelist.

The notion of categorization has always had appeal. Nancy Mitford divided the world into "U" (upper class) and "Non-U"; Lenny Bruce did the same but with Jew and non-Jew. I have always thought that Roth's novels could be divided into "good-boy" books and "bad-boy" books—*Portnoy"* being Roth's most famous bad-boy book; *The Ghost Writer* his best-known good-boy book.

Although the protagonist of *Everyman* may not be a good man (he is estranged from some of his children and treated some of his former wives cruelly), it is a good-boy book, reminding us of how suddenly sickness and death can come to dominate our life narrative. In *Everyman,* the death force is not to be denied.

By contrast, *Sabbath's Theater,* my favorite Roth novel of his recent hot streak, is about Mickey Sabbath, a character so awful, so debauched and degraded yet in whom the life force rages. So it seems, at least with Roth, that in the bad-boy books, the life force commits outrageous acts of defiance, while in the good-boy books (*American Pastoral* comes to mind, as well), the death force wins out—as it does sometimes in life, as well.

Sometimes, we mourn those we barely know or those we know best by the literary works they gave to world. Wendy Wasserstein, who died Jan. 30, 2006, was someone I had met on occasion—she was a contributor to a publication my wife worked for—but did not know. But having seen so many of her plays, such as *Isn't It Romantic* or *The Sisters Rosensweig,* I, like so many others, was a fan. Her untimely death at age fifty-five, a single mother leaving a young child, deeply affected me (or to put it in less literary terms, really bummed me out).

Wasserstein also left behind a first novel, *Elements of Style* (Knopf). Published a few weeks after her death, it is a post-September 11 tale of adultery among New York high society. Shallow person that I am, I had little trouble identifying many of the real-life counterparts from the gossip columns.

Wasserstein may have thought she had found 21st century incarnations of Edith Wharton characters—but let's not forget "The House of Mirth" was anything but uplifting. Here, much to my regret, the life force wrestles the death force to a draw in a novel that, although compelling, was unsatisfying.

The sadness I felt after reading Roth's and Wasserstein's new novels sent me racing to re-read one of the most life-affirming and enjoyable novels I know: *Happy All the Time* by Laurie Colwin (HarperPerennial, 1978), a book I have often given as a gift to friends going through a rough patch. A tale of two couples and their ups and downs, *Happy All the Time* has a charm that is hard to resist and is filled with great lines like: "Sometimes I think it's love, and sometimes I think it's sickness."

Colwin also died too young in 1992 at age forty-eight of a heart attack in her sleep, also leaving behind a young daughter. A few years ago, Jonathan Yardley wrote a great tribute to Colwin and to *Happy All the Time* in the Washington Post, which does her greater justice than I can, in which he called the novel "a wise, big-hearted book by a wise, big-hearted writer."

Perhaps in this summer when the caped wonder has returned, we would be wise to remember the words of Don Juan in George Bernard Shaw's 1903 play *Man and Superman*: "The life force is stupid; but it is not so stupid as the forces of Death and Degeneration. Besides, these are in its pay all the time. And so Life wins, after a fashion."

July 19, 2006

THE MAD ADVENTURES OF GERARD OURY

"The King of popular comedy is dead," proclaimed Le Figaro after Gerard Oury, one of France's most successful directors (if not its most successful) died on Thursday, July 20, at his home in St. Tropez.

I know Oury's work because as a teenager I went with my mother to New York's 68th Street Playhouse, an art house, to see a film called "The Mad Adventures of Rabbi Jacob." A French comedy about a rabbi? Seemed like a contradiction in terms.

The 1973 film is about a rich French racist, played by Luis de Funes, who on his way to attend his daughter's wedding becomes unwittingly involved in a plot to murder an Arab leader and must disguise both himself and the leader as Chasidic rabbis in order to escape. It makes fun of Arab-Jewish relations, anti-Semitism, French snobbery and racism, treating such serious subjects with a light touch. Personally, what I recall is falling out of my chair laughing.

Born Max Gerard Houry Tannenbaum in Paris in 1919, Oury's father was a classical violinist and his mother a journalist for Paris Soir. He began his career as an actor and was accepted as a member of the Comedie Francaise, but fled Vichy France during the German occupation, spending the war years in Switzerland.

Returning to Paris in 1945, he resumed his career as a stage and film actor. He also worked as a screenwriter, receiving a credit on the original *The Mirror Has Two Faces,* which would be remade by Barbra Streisand in 1996.

In 1962, Oury turned to directing and made a series of thrillers, most notably *Le Crime ne Paie Pas* (*Crime Doesn't Pay*), which features the actress Michele Morgan, who would become his life partner, and Louis de Funes, who would become a longtime onscreen collaborator.

It was de Funes who suggested that Oury try his hand at comedy, which he did to great success.

Oury's 1966 comedy *La Grande Vadrouille,* which starred de Funes and Terry Thomas, was released in America as *Don't Look Now, We're Being Shot At.* Thomas starred as a World War II bombardier shot down over Paris who escapes to the South of France with the help of two bumbling French civilians. Call it a "Resistance comedy." According to Variety, it sold 17 million tickets in France, a record that remained unchallenged until 1998 when it was surpassed by "Titanic."

Oury's other films included *Le Cerveau (The Brain), L'as des As (Ace of Aces)* both with Jean-Louis Belmondo, and *La Folie des Grandeurs" (Delusions of Grandeur)* with Yves Montand and Luis de Funes. As reported in Variety, "Oury's six most successful pictures totaled over 50 million tickets in theaters."

Oury directed his last film, *Le Schpountz* in 1999, a remake. His daughter, Danielle Thompson, who co-authored many of his most famous screenplays (including *Rabbi Jacob*), is a successful director and screenwriter in her own right, most famous in America for her screenplay for *Cousin, Cousine.* Oury is remembered for his conviction that no subject was taboo for comedy. But more than that, he believed that in making fun of serious subjects, we could come to understand them, and each other, better.

Watching *Rabbi Jacob* again several years ago, I didn't find it funny anymore. More benign and shtick-filled than I recalled, I found it overburdened by de Funes' mugging and over-acting (exactly the things that made me laugh as a teenager). But watching it last night, I was surprised by the attention and affection Oury lavished on Jewish life and ritual in the film.

The notion that Jews and Arabs should acknowledge each other as cousins—albeit distant ones—with respect, and that France's future lay in embracing Jews and Muslims is all the more remarkable given that the film appeared in 1973, after Munich, and at the time of the Yom Kippur war.

The conceit of *Rabbi Jacob,* that an anti-Semite and an Arab would respect Jews by living among them (and would want to live in peace with them afterward) was strikingly original and comic at the time. Today, this notion of living in someone else's shoes, so to speak, is the basis for several reality programs, from *Wife Swap* to Morgan Spurlock's *30 Days* (in whose first episode a Minuteman lives among a family of illegal Mexican immigrants), to an Israeli version of *Wife Swap* in which an Arab-Israeli and Israeli right-winger trade homes.

Watching *Rabbi Jacob* last night, I didn't feel like I was watching a comedy. Given the recent news, I felt like I was watching a long ago dream—of a time when anti-Semites were funny vaudeville characters, Jews just wanted to be understood for the warm and fuzzy people they were and Arab leaders were just a handshake away from living in peace with their Jewish neighbors.

For that reason alone, I mourn the loss of Gerard Oury.

August 4, 2006

KAPLAN'S COLLAGE

Here's Marty Kaplan blogging on Huffington Post about suggested treatments for Mel Gibson's "problem":

"*Jew Like Me* is another strategy. Walk a mile in my shoes. Gain ten pounds at my table. Wait two hours after lunch before swimming. Laugh that ironic meta-laugh right along with us when Jon Stewart says, 'Jewey.' Sensitize yourself to code like *New York Times* and 'neocon.' Defend Likud. Like halvah. Who knows—you might even get a development deal out of it. *Gentleman's Agreement* meets *Dude, Where's My Foreskin?* If I were Bob Iger, I'd buy that in a New York minute."

You might not guess from reading the above that Kaplan is often referred to as a "public intellectual." But he is. His current title is dean of the Annenberg School at USC and chairman of the Norman Lear Center. But Kaplan has led many lives—molecular biologist, comedy writer, White House speechwriter, Disney exec, radio host. As Kaplan recently wrote me in an e-mail when I asked, "Which of those is you ?"

"I'm all those things, plus father, citizen, liberal, gadfly, civic activist, romantic, Jew, philosophical hypochondriac..."

From my limited exposure I can also add that he is engaging and disarming, with great reserves of charm. So who is Marty Kaplan?

Kaplan was born in Newark, NJ—Philip Roth country—and grew up in the nearby suburb of Union. The grandson of Russian immigrants, Kaplan's father was an accountant whose mother was herself an immigrant from the same Russian shtetl that his grandparents came from. Yiddish was spoken in the home, and the only household Kaplan remembers seeing books was in that of his uncle (his mother's brother), who attended Yale and was a microbiologist.

For his part, Kaplan graduated Harvard College with a summa in molecular biology and worked in the lab of James D. Watson (of Watson and Crick DNA fame). During his time at Harvard, Kaplan was not only president of the Harvard Lampoon (and the first to invite women to join), but also served on the editorial boards of the Crimson, the Advocate and belonged to the Signet Society. When I asked how such multiculturalism could occur, Kaplan replied, "It was during the revolution, so all things were possible."

Kaplan's post-graduate resume is just as impressive: A Marshall Scholarship to Cambridge, where he studied English literature under George Steiner and first befriended Arianna Stassinopoulos (now Huffington) and Douglas Adams of *Hitchhiker's Guide to the Galaxy* fame; followed by a Danforth at Stanford, where his doctoral dissertation in modern thought and philosophy was a study of collage as a way to "build a life out of pieces" in a post-modern world. Which is exactly what Kaplan proceeded to do in his professional life.

Kaplan went to Washington at the start of the Carter administration, serving on the staff of U.S. Commissioner on Education Ernie Boyle before being recruited by Vice President Walter Mondale to be his chief speechwriter.

"I was twenty-seven years old, and I went to work in the White House every day, and I had a front-row seat on history," Kaplan now says.

During his time at 1600 Pennsylvania Ave., he met many future notables, including Bill Clinton, then a first-term governor of Arkansas. Presidential speechwriters included James Fallows (now at the *Atlantic)*, Chris Matthews (*Hardball*) and Hendrik Hertzberg (now at the *New Yorker*). Kaplan hired Charles Krauthammer, who had been a psychiatrist, to his staff.

Carter's presidency was a difficult time with high interest rates, inflation, a gas crisis and the Iran hostage crisis, which kept the president a prisoner in the Rose Garden for 444 days.

"It was hard and dispiriting," Kaplan recalls.

However, as a result, Mondale took on more international assignments. One of Kaplan's proudest moments came when Mondale was called upon to give a speech at the United Nations in Geneva about "the boat people," urging the member nations to take in more Vietnamese refugees. Mondale asked Kaplan to confer with a member of the U.S. delegation, Elie Wiesel, who admonished, "History will be watching you, young man."

"No one would have listened to me if I gave that speech," Kaplan says. But after Mondale spoke, the other nations agreed to help. Wiesel gave Kaplan a hug. That speech, Kaplan says, "made a difference."

In 1980, Carter/Mondale suffered a stinging defeat to Ronald Reagan. In 1984 Mondale campaigned for president. Kaplan was deputy campaign manager and that, too, was a long, hard struggle that ended in defeat.

By the end of 1984, Kaplan had spent eight years in Washington, and California beckoned: He wanted to revive his creative side (that part that presided over the *Lampoon*), and he was envious of his former college roommate, Tom Werner, who had gone to California right out of college to become a successful TV creative executive (and would go on to greater success with Carsey-Werner, *The Cosby Show* and the Boston Red Sox).

Disney Studios had recently been taken over by a new management team: Michael Eisner, Jeffrey Katzenberg and Frank Wells. Katzenberg, who had worked for New York Mayor John Lindsay, saw the analogy between the political and studio worlds and "thought it was worth rolling the dice on me."

Kaplan spent twelve years at Disney, the first five as a vice president at a time when "the entire senior administration could sit on Jeffrey's couch, and we did."

"It was bliss to be part of a group that felt it was reinventing the studio system." Kaplan says.

However Wells' death in 1994 prompted change both in the executive ranks and among the relationship of the executives who remained. What had once been a familiar place became less so to Kaplan, who segued into an exclusive writing and producing deal at Disney. The frustration of working on projects and notes for successive sets of executives wore thin.

"It underscored the arbitrariness of power," he said.

Once again serendipity came knocking in the form of Geoffrey Cowan, who had just been named dean of the Annenberg School at USC. The school was in need of a new direction, leadership and energy. Over breakfast at Junior's, sparks began to fly: "I felt the same excitement I had not felt since my early days at Disney, or my early days at the White House. It felt beshert. So I joined him."

Kaplan is now in the beginning of his tenth year as associate dean of the Annenberg School. Since 2000, he has been director of the Norman Lear Center, "a multidisciplinary research and public policy center exploring the implications of the convergence of entertainment, commerce and society."

What this really means is a convergence of all of Kaplan's myriad interests—the center's manifesto quotes Plato, Aristotle, Dickens, MTV and Neil Postman. As Kaplan sees it, everything today is becoming entertainment, including news and politics. The collage of modern life, if you will.

"For better or for worse, the need to capture and hold the attention of audiences is at the core of practically every domain in modern society," he said.

Over the past few years, Annenberg has partnered with the Centers for Disease Control and Prevention to provide experts and information to writers and producers so that the medical information presented on such shows as *Grey's Anatomy* or a daytime soap opera is accurate (Are you really surprised that people find out about diseases and treatments from TV programs?)

The Lear Center has supported studies and publications examining how politics and propaganda were promulgated by Warner Bros. during wartime, as well as discussions on the ownership of creative content and on the image of the journalist in American film, to name but a few of the dozens of projects the center has initiated. Among the projects Kaplan is most proud of is a study of global TV and the public interest obligations of local TV news, as well as symposia and publications asking how to improve political coverage on TV, particularly on local news programs.

Kaplan's resume as redacted in this column could be read as a series of unrelated career moves. But ask him how he sees what he's doing, and he answers: "What I'm trying to do is tikkun olam, to illuminate and repair the world, to shine a moral, political, academic light on consequential currents moving in our world in this lifetime. To make people think, to laugh, and to act."

August 17, 2006

THE RETURN OF THE PLAYER

The fall season is upon us, with new books, movies and TV programs all vying for our attention as palliatives to the news of war, terrorism and melting ice caps. Even as the days get shorter and our own day of judgment looms imminent, we wonder: Is there a hero out there who can set us back on the path of reason, on a course of love, someone to heal us and show us the way—someone, who is, in the words of Lermontov, "a hero of our time?" Yes, as a matter of fact, there is.

All hail Griffin Mill and *The Return of the Player*, by Michael Tolkin. Eighteen years ago, in *The Player*, Tolkin introduced us to Griffin Mill, a studio executive who gets away with murder—literally. Tolkin's successful novel was followed in 1992 by a Robert Altman film version, for which Tolkin wrote the Oscar-nominated screenplay.

Since then, Tolkin, who is now fifty-five, has published two other novels, *Among the Dead* and *Under Radar*, directed two movies, *The Rapture* and *The New Age*, for which he also wrote the screenplays, and he has received credit on several successful produced movies, including *Sudden Impact* and *Changing Lanes*. He's also written and rewritten many other screenplays.

Now Griffin Mill is back, and despite his past crime, he wants to bring people together—to have them connect honestly and ethically. He says, "I know you, and I know what you want." Griffin Mill has changed.

If *The Player* was very much a novel of manners, of the customs of Hollywood, *The Return of The Player* is a novel of ideas, with Tolkin taking creative leaps to express his many thoughts and theories on everything from teenagers (and yes, he has read the work of clinical psychologist and author Wendy Mogul, his wife), family love, marriage, Moses versus Homer (or that "the structure of Greek legends make good movies and the structure of Jewish legends make mediocre TV series"), to what Bill Clinton could and should have said.

I sat down recently with Tolkin in his Hancock Park office to talk about the return of *The Player,* and I found that, like Griffin Mill, Tolkin has a lot on his mind.

Our conversation veered from the state of the movie industry and movies to Abu Ghraib and the end of the American myth of a code of honor, to Tolkin's experience with a Wexner fellowship studying Judaism, to changes in Reform liturgical services, to reasons for optimism in a world of pain—or, at least, reasons not to despair.

Tolkin's insider cred is both earned and inherited. His father, Mel Tolkin, wrote his way from musical theatricals and summer Pocono Camp Tamiment sketch revues to head writer of Sid Caesar's *Show of Shows,* where his now-legendary writing staff included Lucille Kallen (Mel Tolkin's former writing partner), Neil and Danny Simon, Mel Brooks and Woody Allen. Michael Tolkin's mother was a vice president of legal affairs at Paramount.

The Tolkin family moved to Los Angeles from New York when Michael was ten. He became bar mitzvah at Temple

Emanuel and graduated from Beverly Hills High School. Tolkin then went back east to attend Middlebury College. After graduating, he returned to New York, where he worked as a journalist for such publications as The Village Voice, before returning to Los Angeles to embark on a screenwriting career.

By the late 1980s, Tolkin was a working screenwriter. His script for *Gleaming the Cube* (released in 1989 and now a skateboarding cult classic) was about to be made when he got an idea that, as he recalled , "didn't feel like a movie." "I had never had that happen before," Tolkin said. He explained that within the first few pages he had a character in a dilemma, and that the way it works for him, in the four times he has had ideas for novels, "the dilemma becomes a question and then an organizing principle."

The Player reads today, much as it did when originally published, as a polished literary effort—more like Daniel Fuchs' *The Golden West* than Nathaniel West's *Day of the Locust*—a novel by someone who knew the lay of the land and despite it was going to stay in Hollywood.

What *The Player* had going for it was a sense of the real—it took for granted that this was the way the game was played and was neither dismissive nor critical; it just told the facts. Yet by putting Griffin Mill in the center of the story, it presented Hollywood as a world that stood apart from morality, a concept that met with no resistance. Griffin Mill came to embody Hollywood in his day, much as Ari Gold on *Entourage* does today.

So imagine my surprise when Tolkin revealed that "The model for Griffin was never anything in Hollywood." Turns out Tolkin found his inspiration in Washington, D.C.

"It was Eliott Abrams lying during the Iran-Contra hearing,"

Tolkin confided. "That's who it explicitly was—but only to the degree that watching Eliot Abrams lie at the time, I wondered: What had happened to guilt? How can this guy sleep at night? Then I started to think about the ways in which 19th century guilt was a matter of the soul; early twentieth century guilt was a matter of psychology. Now guilt had become more a neurotic tick than anything profound. Some people really didn't have it. We were a sociopathic culture. And then I went from there."

"*The Return of the Player*, is a sequel only in the loosest sense. First of all, it has very little to do with the Hollywood of studios and movie making. But it has everything to with living in Los Angeles at this particular moment in the tweny-first century, and that is intentional.

Tolkin explained that the idea for *The Return of The Player* came to him about four years ago, when he was having a conversation with a producer about an executive who was broke. Although Tolkin understood broke to mean out of money, somehow the phrase "down to his last couple of million" came into the conversation. Later, as Tolkin sat in the chair in his office, the opening sentence came to him, "Griffin Mill was broke; he was down to his last $6 million."

"I started working on it really from that idea," he recalled. "It all came to me: That he was fifty-two... It took me half a page before I found out that he was remarried, that he was divorced from June, and that his wife wanted a divorce from him. The first twenty-five or thirty pages I wrote in about ten days, and they haven't changed significantly in the four years since I started working on the book." "What I wanted to write was a novel about Los Angeles, not about Hollywood. I wanted to write a book which took for granted that people understood what The

Grove was, what boba was, what neighborhoods were, what waiting in line at the ArcLight was like. I wanted to write a really local novel. I wanted to write about private schools for kids and teenagers and avoid what I think is pretty much exhausted, the story of Hollywood."

For Griffin, movies are about heroes, and the structure of movies is about the hero's journey, a fact any development exec who has read Christopher Vogler's *The Writer's Journey,* which purports to apply the principles of Joseph Campbell to three-act screenplay structure, can tell you. In the novel, Griffin decides to leave the movie business and make himself the hero of his own journey. He allies himself with Phil Ginsburg, a near billionaire who wants to reach the next level of wealth, all in the pursuit of finding a safe haven for his family, his two wives, and three children, in a world that he fears is about to end.

So why does Griffin believe Hollywood is dying?

"One of the things that Griffin understands is that the movies are dead," Tolkin said, "because the myths are gone, because the myths are dead. Once everybody analyzes the structure behind myths, and you're watching a movie and the movie is deconstructed and broken apart before you, you can't follow the narrative. You are following the structure and that's not entertaining. The movies can't take you out of yourself."

Tolkin told me that after he finished the novel, he spent the summer "going to the movies and walking out of the movies and not going to the movies." As he talked to his friends who were doing the same, "especially people in Hollywood who don't go to the movies anymore," he found that "there's no joy in the movies." At meetings, people no longer talked about what movie they saw over the weekend, except to say how disappointed or disinterested they were. What they talked about was "The Sopranos."

Tolkin mentioned that his nineteen-year-old daughter "hates the movies," adding that, "She hates the movies in a way that I hated Lawrence Welk when I was fifteen. She dismisses the movies."

Tolkin's explanation: "The movies used to be about characters. Characters have migrated to television... The quality of the writing, the quality of the acting, the quality of the storytelling, it's much more interesting on TV."

Television is compelling, Tolkin feels, because it is about family. By contrast, he said, "there may be movies with individual moments of heroism, but the idea of the hero is finished, and that was killed by Abu Ghraib."

"The thing that changed America, which also changed popular culture, was Abu Ghraib," he said. "With Abu Ghraib, the American myth of its own superiority was destroyed. Its own idealism was destroyed."

"Abu Ghraib expressed the result of something that was happening in the culture for a long time," Tolkin said, "which is the coarsening, the hardening, the introduction of cruelty."

"Even though soldiers have been cruel—America has been racist; the Indians were killed—there was an ideal, a code, Humphrey Bogart, Bob Dylan, the outlaw. There was a code of honor that one lived up to. Because the Constitution describes a code of honor: You live and let live, you respect each other. Even if we hadn't been doing that, it was something to aspire to, and it was a myth you could keep returning to."

But Tolkin feels that myth has fallen by the wayside: "In the way that Zeus is a myth. A lot of people used to believe in Zeus, and that fell apart, another story came in. A revolution is a story that becomes a myth that becomes an organizing principle."

"The movies can only express...different attributes and different aspects and different ways of thinking about that organizing principle in a culture; and that organizing principle in this country is finished or really, really sick.

"TV is interesting because [it shows us] all the fragmentation and the effect on the family in society. It's like dreams, if you look at TV, from *The Office* to *Deadwood*, *The Sopranos*, '*The O.C.*, *Lost*, [each of these is] a picture of a family. The doctor shows and cops shows have characters who are essentially decent and untouched by history, untouched by current events. They live in a bubble of idealism. But everywhere else, you see the effects of the culture."

For example, Tolkin said, "The reality shows [show] the naked competitiveness, the squalid selfishness and the process of elimination. That's pretty brutal. The hero is the one that survives, by what? By cheating? By organizing? By getting rid of the others? By politicking, by sneaking..."

"That's a different myth than what we used to have. That's a different story," Tolkin concludes.

"And that's what my novel is about. That's what I wrote. That's why I wrote it. Because I was thinking of all these things, and I wanted to—express that." But tell us, Michael: What do you really think?

As my head was reeling from Tolkin's searing exegesis, I, too, realized what the *Return of the Player* is about—getting one's panic under control by becoming the master of your own fate and taking responsibility for being connected to your family. As good a recipe for living in the modern world as any, because if you can do that, you can feel much better about the world and your place in it.

Griffin Mill is fifty-two, and he is panicked, as many of us are, because he works for a studio that he will never run; his family are all alienated—everyone hiding out in his or her own private space; and the world itself is out of control. His only solution is to attempt to create a happy ending out of a potential tragedy. As Tolkin explained, the other key to understanding *The Return of The Player* is the Edith Wharton quote that prefaces the novel that "Americans want a tragedy with a happy ending."

This, too, is Tolkin's mission. *The Return of The Player* is filled with improbable plot turns, leaps of faith, leaps of folly, scenes and speeches that defy our expectations of where the story will lead—culminating in moments of sheer chutzpah, that like the novel's hero, lead us to a happy ending.

When I asked Tolkin how Bill Clinton comes to make a cameo in the novel, after joking that it was paid product placement, Tolkin said, "I was trying to imagine something wonderful. It's one of these things where you're sitting at your desk, and you have a great cackle of pleasure, an idea bubbling out of the cosmos: Here, have him talk to Clinton."

Tolkin continued, "I wanted to give Griffin the happiest ending possible. I think, given the state of the world right now, given the nostalgic fantasy that but for the blue dress Clinton would have solved the world's problem, talking to Clinton to try to understand the world in which we live right now, who wouldn't want to do that? If you have that fantasy [as many do]." Plus, Tolkin admitted, "I wanted Clinton to say what I've always wanted him to say."

But beyond explaining himself, his marriage and his actions, Clinton becomes Griffin's confessor, and then leads him to consider King David "who sent Uriah into battle to die so he could marry Bathsheba." And what Clinton has to say about King David has a profound effect on Griffin, leading to the novel's surprising conclusion.

Which leads me to a different point. In our conversation, Tolkin told me, "Griffin's thinking more...Part of his panic is that he's got an expanded consciousness, and he's frightened."

In the years since the publication of *The Player,* Tolkin's consciousness has also expanded, in part from his studies as a Wexner fellow, a program seeded by retail magnate Leslie Wexner, which aims to educate potential Jewish volunteer leaders from diverse backgrounds in Jewish history and the challenges facing the Jewish community.

Tolkin grew up in a home that was not particularly observant, like many families that belonged to Reform synagogues in the 1950s. By the early 1990s, he belonged to three temples: the Orthodox B'nai David-Judea, the Conservative Temple Beth Am and the Reform Temple Israel of Hollywood. He was studying with Rabbi Danny Landes, who is a faculty member of The Wexner Foundation, when he was invited to apply to become a fellow. For Tolkin, "The great thing about Wexner was the study." It is a program where one can learn from teachers from all over the spectrum, from historians to Reform and Orthodox scholars.

"What I discovered for myself, what drew me to studying with the Orthodox, was the discovery that the Reform prayer book had the prayers in Hebrew, but the translation was at best free form, and at worst inaccurate. When I discovered Artscroll [a publishing imprint of Jewish texts translated from an Orthodox perspective], I started looking at the more stringent translations, and I discovered a poetry and a structure in Jewish prayer that I never felt before." Tolkin noted that today, many congregations are creating their own new prayer books with renewed love for and emphasis on liturgy, which he sees as one of the greatest changes and improvements for "Klal Yisroel and the Galut."

Griffin Mill isn't Jewish, but his wife Lisa is, as is his partner, Phil Ginsburg, who stages a lavish bar mitzvah for his son. His outsider status allows Griffin to be an observer at events that other Jews might sit in judgment of. He is not searching for a spirituality that will force him to feel guilty, rather he is looking for a way to be honest—and to connect.

Although Tolkin asserts that there is nothing about the events of the last four years that would make Griffin any less panicked, it also true that there is nothing that would make Griffin, and by that measure Tolkin himself, not embark on a journey to renounce that panic.

I can't say that I really know Michael Tolkin, although we went to the same college—Middlebury—and while our years there did overlap, we didn't know each other then. Coincidentally, in the years since graduation we have both made contributions to the college aimed at improving Jewish life there. Still, here and there, over the years, I've run into him, often at gatherings in support of Jewish causes.

I am always reading and hearing about how Hollywood refuses to support Israel or that Jews "are afraid to come out of the closet on Israel," but in my experience that is not the case. As Mel Gibson well knows, the International Jewish Conspiracy does meet on occasion, and over the years I have found myself in the same room, event or meeting as Michael Tolkin. He has written for *The Jewish Journal of Greater Los Angeles,* speaking out forcefully against anti-Semitism, and presenting his drashes on matters secular and biblical, dressing down narrow-minded conservatives and fundamentalists, and shining some light for the rest of us wandering in the desert of modern America.

On some of those occasions, I have observed that Tolkin seemed to be under a dark cloud. So I asked him if, like Griffin, during the writing of the novel the balance had shifted between his own pessimism and optimism. He quipped, "Yeah, but I won't tell you which way."

But as we discussed reasons for optimism in a world of worry, Tolkin said the following: "Judaism teaches that despair is really a sin. That's as important a teaching as any. We have a couple of days a year proscribed for mourning, and that's it. And you don't bury somebody on Shabbos."

To put it another way: Jewish tradition and storytelling is partial to the well-articulated kvetch. However, for a story with a happy ending, you'll have to turn to Griffin Mill and *The Return of The Player.*

September 14, 2006

WALK LIKE A ROCKSTAR MOM

"Hannah Montana," a Disney Channel program I watch on occasion with my daughter, features a fourteen-year-old girl with a secret identity: she's actually a rock star. This is an absurd fantasy.

In real life, the rock star at my daughter's school is a mom. Although she leads a double life, it is no secret. Her name is Susanna Hoffs, her band The Bangles has a long history (hits, breakup, back together again), and she also has a very enjoyable a new album with Matthew Sweet, *Under The Covers, Vol. 1* that consists of glossy reworkings of 1960s chestnuts, such as "Different Drum" or "Who Knows Where the Time Goes," as well as other classics and rarities from The Beatles, Neil Young, Bob Dylan and The Who.

Most days, Hoffs, like the other moms, is dropping off her kids at school or attending gatherings and parent conferences. But this Friday, as this article appears in print, she will perform with The Bangles at a school assembly. It's good to live in Los Angeles.

Over the summer, as Hoffs performed with Matthew Sweet and toured with The Bangles, there was a moment when I was afraid I was turning into her stalker. I was staying up late to watch her on Jay Leno (and even later on Conan); pulling over on Sunset to listen to her on Jonesy's Jukebox on Indie 103.1 FM; I was standing in a crowd at the Roxy to hear her perform; and hanging out at Yahoo!'s music studio as she and Sweet recorded an "in studio" performance and interview (thanks to Bob Roback, head of Yahoo! music). But my doctor adjusted my medication, and he says it's under control now.

Here's what I find so striking: Hoffs is totally at home on stage, in platform heels and minidress, playing her "Susanna Hoffs" model Rickenbacker electric guitar. In some ways, Hoffs appears more at ease on stage than she does in person—at school and in the neighborhood.

Recently, when I asked Hoffs about this, she described the transition from mom to being on stage as being like Peter Parker transforming into Spider-Man. "It's another persona," she said.

All of which begs the obvious: How did a nice Jewish girl from Santa Monica become a rock star?

Hoffs describes herself as a kid who was into music, theater, art and movies and, who, by elementary school, already had a passion to be in a band. Growing up, her neighbor worked at Capitol Records and provided Hoffs' family with all the Beatles albums (and yes, Paul was her favorite). Her mother's brother had a musical instrument store and gave her guitar lessons. Her first band was posing with her older and younger brothers.

The first records she bought were Carole King's *Tapestry* and James Taylor's *Sweet Baby James*. "Déj? vu" by Crosby Stills, Nash & Young came soon after. Hoffs recalls that in high school she wore out her copy of Joni Mitchell's *Court and Spark* and was into Bonnie Raitt.

At UC Berkeley, Hoffs continued her artistic journey. She was in a dance company, and started out as a dance major before switching to fine arts. She finally graduated as a theater arts major. During college she also had her first band, a duo with David Roback, later of Mazzy Starr (no relation to Yahoo!'s Bob). Hoffs describes that group as "John and Yoko meet The Beach Boys." Hoffs came to believe, and still believes, that "being in a band is the ultimate art project."

After college she moved back to Los Angeles. She bought an electric guitar from The Recycler (the Craigslist of its day). Answering another Recycler ad looking for a guitarist led to forming a band with several other women, and that, in 1981, became The Bangles.

Meanwhile, Hoffs was supporting herself through a variety of jobs. She had a relative who made ceramics, and she worked in the ceramics factory. She also worked for a company that offered diamond chips as part of its promotions—which really meant that Hoffs spent her time packing UPS boxes, preparing the invoices and shipping the diamonds. All the while she was listening to K-Earth 101 FM, the oldies station.

Success did not come overnight. "We started out playing out on the outskirts in Arcadia, deep in the Valley. We worked our way towards Hollywood," she said. It was a slow build.

Hoffs recalled some of the landmarks, or "OMYGOD" moments: The first time they heard their own song played on the radio ("Getting Out of Hand," self-released and played by KROQ DJ Rodney Bingenheimer); being signed to Columbia Records; quitting her day job; standing on a street corner and hearing "Manic Monday" playing from a car ("It was shocking"); opening for The English Beat and for Cyndi Lauper; playing enormous festivals in Europe before audiences of 100,000. "And we felt like we were a little garage band from L.A," she said.

"Another OMYGOD moment was opening for Queen and just walking out on the stage and looking out at the crowd," she recalled. "Surreal is the best way to describe it."

And there was Hoffs' "Dolce Vita" moment at a press conference at the Sanremo Music Festival in Italy, where there were hundreds of photographers. Later, that night the guys from Duran Duran invited them for dinner, and there were girls, hundreds of girls, climbing all over the car, banging on the windows, with Duran Duran casually ignoring all the fuss.

"It was so funny," she said.

It would be easy to say that the success of The Bangles owed a great deal to being attractive females playing pop tunes. But their appeal was more punk, more emotional.

The bands that inspired Hoffs, such as The Velvet Underground, The Talking Heads, Television and Blondie were all considered art bands. To some extent they were also New York bands, born out of the cauldron of clubs like Max's Kansas City and CBGB's. Hoffs embraced that aesthetic—she is proud to recount that she attended the Sex Pistols' legendary last performance in San Francisco—but she gave the form another twist, a California-bred sensibility. The songs The Bangles wrote and performed, and the 1960s classics they covered, all shared what Hoffs characterizes as "pop melodies with a dark side."

In the 1970s, California rock (Jackson Browne, CSN&Y, The Eagles) took the 1960s' New York coffee house folk movement and added a layer of emotional wistfulness, a chord of melancholy to the otherwise cloudless California days. Similarly, what The Bangles did in the 1980s was to take sixties pop harmonies and infuse them with an edge, both musically and emotionally (case in point: listen to "Hero Takes a Fall" or their cover of

Simon and Garfunkel's "Hazy Shade of Winter" from the *Less Than Zero* soundtrack).

The Bangles broke up in 1989. The details have been memorialized in a VH1 "Behind the Music," which is worth watching just for the parade of eighties hairstyles. What Hoffs says now is, "We needed to go off and have our own lives."

Hoffs says that when you are young a band becomes your family, and that at a certain point: "It was part of our growing-up process. We had to rebel against each other."

Hoffs spent the 1990s pursuing solo projects. She also married Jay Roach, and they became the parents of those two children who are the reason I see Hoffs around school. Roach, who during that decade went from TV writer-producer to one of the most successful directors in Hollywood (*Austin Powers, Meet the Parents*), is also partly responsible for the events leading to The Bangles' reunion (Roach asked Hoffs to write a song for the Austin Powers sequel, for which she enlisted her former bandmates' help, after which they played at a 1999 Beatles tribute before formally reuniting in 2000); Hoffs' current collaboration with Matthew Sweet (he was part of Ming Tea, the Mike Meyers/Austin Powers band); and for another OMYGOD moment—performing at the Oscars for a billion people ("My heart was beating like in a cartoon," Hoffs recalled).

Hoffs said that being a Bangle again "is very fun." What she came to realize is that "if you are in a band for a long time, you have a sound." It was a sound that she realized she couldn't make with others.

She said that audiences have "a certain appreciation for what we do that's grown." Hoffs explained that she feels good that The Bangles decided to work together again, and she is happy because it seems to mean something to people. At the same time, Hoffs sees playing with Matthew Sweet as "a chance to enjoy making music in a different way." There are already plans for a Vol. 2 of covers, this time from the 1970s. Hoffs feels that "when you do a cover song," it brings it into the culture again, "giving a new generation of kids a chance to access the song."

Which is exactly what The Bangles will do when they perform this Friday. I'll just have to explain to my daughter that while *Hannah Montana* isn't real, Susanna Hoffs is...She's the real deal—all mom/part rock star.

September 28, 2006

RUBIN'S WAR

To meet him, you might think Steven Rubin is a normal person. Tall, handsome, happily married with young children, he is personable, affable—in short, one of the gentlest and nicest guys you could meet. But he is a man obsessed with war—World War II to be precise.

Recently, Rubin launched www.ww2daily.com, a Web site that posts a daily broadcast of the news that occurred on that day during World War II. Rubin began posting his broadcasts on September 11, 2006, with the news from September 11, 1939, and he intends to go day by day for the next six years, until he reaches VJ day, September 2, 1945—in 2012.

"My vision is part entertainment, part history," Rubin said recently, "to tell the story of America at its greatest." Rubin feels this is particularly important today, to remind the world of what America helped accomplish.

Rubin envisions his web site as a broadcast channel devoted to the war, as a site where students, veterans, history buffs and collectors can all interact. He has assembled a team of a dozen writers, including a military historian, a schoolteacher and several professional writers, who scour archives for the actual war news of the day. In addition, there are four editors.

To save costs, Rubin had originally planned to serve as the radio newsreader, but he had to fire himself after he recorded the first few. Instead, he hired stage professional David Cox. Rubin's plan is to eventually hire other correspondents to read the reports as they were filed from various locations and sources. As he refines his business plan, he is currently shoring up investors and advertisers.

Why? You might reasonably ask. The answer is that Rubin wanted to take a shot at making his passion be his business (or make his business be his passion)—it's one or the other or maybe both. Rubin was born in Chicago in 1951. His family moved to Los Angeles in 1955, and Rubin grew up in the Pico-Robertson and Beverlywood neighborhoods.

His fascination with World War II took hold as a child absolutely riveted to Sgt. Rock comic books and to the *Combat!* TV show. One of the first books he ever read was about the Battle of the Bulge, and when he played after school, suddenly the hedges along Robertson in Beverlywood became battlegrounds, where he re-enacted Montgomery's attacks on Rommel.

It was a childhood that included seeing the film about the young Jack Kennedy, *PT 109* (1963), at the Stadium Theater (now the home of B'nai David-Judea Congregation) and *The Longest Day* at the Carthay Circle Theater. One of his favorite films was *The Great Escape,* and one of Rubin's cherished childhood memories is once, at age twelve, meeting Steve McQueen, who was lost and looking for directions to Culver City.

At UCLA, Rubin studied military history by attending ROTC classes (although he never enlisted in ROTC or the armed services). It was also in college that Rubin discovered a talent for writing, joining the UCLA college newspaper, the

Daily Bruin.

Upon graduation, Rubin put his interests to work, writing his first book, *Combat Films* (MacPharland), a study of war movies for which he interviewed his idols, including director John Sturges (*Thunderbolt, The Great Escape*), director Henry Hathaway (*The House on 92nd Street*) and actor Cliff Robertson (*PT 109*).

Writing about movies and movie stars led Rubin to a 20-year career working in publicity, first at the studios and then at Showtime.

Showtime gave Rubin the opportunity to become a producer on *Bleacher Bums* (2002), based on Roberta Custer's successful play of the same name. He also produced *Silent Night* (2002), a fact-based story about a World War II Christmas truce for the Hallmark Channel, which starred Linda Hamilton. Rubin decided to become a full-time producer, but despite his successes, he found that being in production can be elusive. So while continuing to pursue his producing projects (including one with yours truly), Rubin decided that he needed to focus professionally on what he cared about most. Which is when he had his "eureka!" moment, to launch a Web site devoted to World War II.

Which brings me back to the question of "why." Being of the same relative vintage as Rubin, I see the attraction. Although the war occurred long before we were born, for many of our generation, World War II represents a time when things were black and white. When the Americans were the good guys and cheered as they liberated Europe.

Korea? Vietnam? Grenada? Iraq 1? Iraq 2? None have the epic and heroic sweep that we associate with what Tom Brokaw calls, "The Greatest Generation."

That would be the easy answer. Perhaps the more noble one. But I think there's another theory. Rubin is having his midlife crisis—not the bad kind but the good.

Much has been made of the male midlife crisis. Most media depictions of this phenomenon involve the male of the species besotted by small cars with large engines and/or young women with large flotation devices, often mixed together in a combination that disrupts marriages.

While this may be all too real an occurrence, there is a corollary that is rarely reported—a positive version, where a person (and when I say a "person" I really am referring to someone of the male persuasion) decides to give their life greater meaning by changing not their family life but the content of their life.

So, for example, a Bill Gates decides to devote himself to charity, or an Arnold Schwarzenegger takes up politics and becomes governor of California. These are but a few famous examples. Among my friends, some have found religion late in life; others have decided to pursue their avocations as photographers, artists, novelists.

As I see it, these are not unrelated occurrences. Whether motivated by altruism or narcissism, ego or just plain fear of death—each is seeking, in their own way, a greater meaning and a connection to something larger than themselves. Rubin, for his part, is making World War II come alive at his Web site.

"We have a beachhead," Rubin says, "I would like us to be the MySpace for World War II buffs—anyone from a 14-year-old video gamer to an 80-year-old war veteran with a lot of baby boomers in between." I say: Why not? Let Rubin win his war. We all sleep better when the good guys triumph.

October 19, 2006

A DIFFERENT ISRAEL

When Israel is discussed these days, more often than not it is in terms of an existential crisis, or "the situation," or as the subject of international news headlines. However, reading recently published works by three different Israeli fiction authors, Etgar Keret, Benjamin Tammuz and A.B. Yehoshua, is a bracing reminder that there is an Israel beyond the headlines, a country that despite its short history and relatively small population has produced a world-class literature.

Writing in modern Hebrew, a language that few read with any fluency (even in Israel), the accomplishment is all the more remarkable. Israel has already produced several generations of great and memorable writers.

A quick greatest hits list would certainly include works by novelists such as S.Y. Agnon (*21 Stories*), who was awarded the Nobel Prize for literature in 1966; Amos Oz (*My Michael, Black Book*); Aharon Appelfeld (*Badenheim 1939*); David Grossman (*See: Under Love*), as well as the poets Byalik and, one of my favorites, the late poet Yehuda Amichai (*Selected Poems* or *Poems of Jerusalem and Love Poems*).

Currently, Keret, born in 1967, is one of Israel's most popular young authors. He has published several collections of short stories in Hebrew, as well as several graphic novels, and has written TV, as well as film scripts. His short stories have inspired some forty short films. This year's Sundance Film Festival presented *Wristcutters: a Love Story* based on Keret's short story, *Kneller's Happy Campers.*

Keret's first English-language short story collection, *The Nimrod Flip Out,* has recently been published in paperback and is a great introduction to his work.

Keret's stories are short, many no longer than a few pages, and feature a deadpan-style that is often surreal or darkly comic. In one story, a man picks up a girl, only to discover that in the middle of the night, she transforms into a hairy-backed, beer-guzzling guy's guy. Although dismayed at first, the narrator eventually realizes he now has the best of both worlds. In another story, a father and mother hate their child's pet dog and try covertly to kill it—but each time the loyal pet returns—albeit a bit more ragged and damaged. Reading Keret's work you have both a sense of the modern world and of the dissonance of so-called normal life in Israel.

By contrast, *The Minotaur,* by Tammuz, who died in 1989, is a much more psychologically intense novel. Tammuz was born in Russia in 1919 and arrived in then Palestine five years later. A diplomat as well as a sculptor, for many years Tammuz was the literary editor of Ha'aretz.

Recently reissued by Europa Editions, *The Minotaur* was originally published in 1981, at which time Graham Greene hailed it as one of the best novels of the year. It is easy to see why it appealed to Greene.

The Minotaur is not a spy novel, per se. However, it is about a spy and the relationship he develops with a young woman he sees on a bus, permeating her life without ever meeting her. His obsession with her creates a psychological prison with no escape for the two of them, causing great collateral damage to her, her fiancé and his own family.

Finally, and this is the case of saving the best for last, the recently published *A Woman in Jerusalem* by Yehoshua may be the best novel I have read this year.

Sometimes you taste a great wine and are immediately aware that what you are tasting is at a whole level of better than anything else you've been tasting. That is what reading *A Woman in Jerusalem* is like.

Yehoshua's novel succeeds at being both entertaining and lyrical. *A Woman in Jerusalem* centers on Yulia, a Soviet immigrant who was the victim of a terrorist bombing. A week has gone by and her body has not been claimed. A muckracking journalist is about to expose her employer, a bakery, for not knowing and not caring. It falls to the human resources manager to discover who this woman was and to restore her dignity.

No one in the novel is ever named, other than Yulia, and she is dead. The human resources manager is our guide on a journey that questions national identity (the woman was a non-Jew, yet became attached to Israel even when her husband and son returned to Russia) and love (a photograph reveals her beauty and the manager discovers how others fell under her spell even as he does).

He must reconsider his relationships with his mother, his ex-wife, his daughter and his secretary. He accompanies the casket back to Russia, undergoing a series of misadventures that are comic, poignant and, in the final analysis, optimistic.

It is not a given that difficult times produce great literature.

But it is a salve and a comfort that reading these novels provide a portal to accessing another Israel, no less important and newsworthy, one that we can travel to just by opening a book.

November 2, 2006

DAVID MAMET HAS A QUESTION FOR THE WICKED SON

David Mamet has written a book, *The Wicked Son: Anti-Semitism, Self-Hatred and the Jews* (Shocken/Nextbook), that is by turns bold, courageous, and outrageous—it is a book that calls Diaspora Jews to the table and asks: "In or Out?"

"The underlying premise of the book," Mamet told me recently, "is to all Jews: If you can't say of your fellow Jews ' my people,' get out of my way; I don't want to know you, because our people are getting murdered, and to posit an exemption because of intellectual differences...is insane."

The Wicked Son is one of those books that, as I was reading it, made me think of all the people I would like to send a copy—a few to friends who would enjoy it, but even more to those friends (or former friends) who might see themselves in Mamet's disquisition on anti-Semitism, including disaffected and disengaged Jews.

Mamet is the playwright who wrote *Glengarry Glen Ross* (for which he won the Pulitzer Prize), as well as *American Buf-*

falo, Speed-the-Plow, Oleanna, and *Boston Marriage*, among many others. He has directed several movies from his own screenplays, including *House of Cards, Heist* and *The Spanish Prisoner,* as well as writing (and re-writing) many other screenplays. He has published three novels, including *The Old Religion* (about the Leo Frank case), as well as children's books and essay collections. He is currently the co-creator and executive producer of *The Unit,* a one-hour dramatic series that airs on CBS on Tuesdays at 9 p.m.

When I spoke with Mamet recently, he explained that he has been pondering the idea of Jewish passivity for fifteen years or so (beginning around the time he made "Homicide," a film about a Jewish policeman and his issues of identity and self-loathing).

The Wicked Son is a reference to the parable told as part of the Passover seder—of four sons, one wise, one wicked, one simple and the other too young to even ask a question. As part of the seder we are told how best to answer these four different responses to the story of the Jews' emancipation from Egypt.

In *The Wicked Son,* Mamet identifies the many contemporary forms of anti-Semitism, unmasks those who support it or who, passively, refuse to stand up against it. "Anti-Semitism is a sickness, and its playbook is extremely limited," he told me. In *The Wicked Son,* he exposes several canards used by anti-Semites of all stripes—double standards, faulty logic—demonstrating that the arguments used by today's anti-Semites haven't changed much throughout Jewish history.

Mamet also believes it is self-loathing that animates Jews who don't glory in their heritage, culture and tradition and who, worse yet, put forward the anti-Semites' own arguments.

Mamet writes that his book is directed, "To the wicked son, who asks ' What does all this mean to you?'; to the Jews who, in the seventies envied the Black Power Movement; who, in the nineties, envied the Palestinians; who weep at *Exodus* but jeer at the Israel Defense Forces; who nod when Tevye praises tradition but fidget through the seder; who might take your curiosity to a dogfight, to a bordello or an opium den, but find ludicrous the notion of a visit to the synagogue; whose favorite Jew is Anne Frank and whose second-favorite does not exist; who are humble in their desire to learn about Kwanzaa and proud of their ignorance of Tu B'Shevat; who dread endogamy more than incest; who bow their head reverently at a baptism and have never attended a bris. To you, who find your religion and race repulsive, your ignorance of your history a satisfaction, here is a book from your brother."

Making your gift list yet?

In less than forty short chapters, Mamet presents his exegeses on a variety of topics, with titles such as *The Other, Bar Mitzvah and Golden Calf, A Rich Shul and a Poor Shul, The Apikoros and Gun Control, Dead Jews and Live Jews, What Israel Means to Me"* and *The Children of Kings and Queens.*

The book is challenging not only in its content, but in its style. Mamet, whose plays' profane, expletive-laden, staccato-like dialogue came to be known as "Mamet-speak," here takes upon a more formal style, more Alan Dershowitz than David Mamet, more like an oration or a theorem proof—you almost expect Mamet to preface his conclusions with an "ergo" or a "quod erat demonstra" (I think there is a nunc pro tunc somewhere in the book). And yet...And yet, the effect of one chapter after another is a sort of a series of whacks to the head—

at the end of which you ask yourself: Isn't he right? Even if I quibble with some of the statements or generalizations, isn't the gestalt dead on—and if so, what is it that I disagree with here?

Mamet is not so much concerned about the reason for anti-Semitism as he is with the fact of it. He frankly acknowledges it, exposes it and confronts it.

"The most chilling thing I have ever seen in a movie is this spectacular documentary, *One Day in September,* about the Munich massacre," Mamet told me. "There's a scene, a long lens shot of one part of the compound that is under siege—it's ringed by the German security police—and inside the ring of the German security police is the building where Arafat's Black September people have kidnapped and are murdering the Jewish athletes. Then the camera pans over 'x' degrees to the right and on the other side of the fence is the Olympic athletes' compound, where you see people swimming in the Olympic pool, diving into the Olympic pool, and playing ping pong and sunning themselves." And that, for Mamet, is the state of world. To this day.

At one point in our conversation, Mamet asked what I thought of the book. I told him that there were moments while reading the book when I wondered if he was crazy (I said crazy, but what I was thinking was "meshugge") but then I would get to the end of the chapter and wonder if he wasn't essentially right. Mamet asked for an example. So I cited the opening of the chapter titled "Well Poisoning." It begins:

"There have always been unstated but universally understood exemptions in human behavior. In this country the poor are permitted adultery and a certain degree of spousal abuse and murder, but are barred from theft; the rich are allowed to steal and take drugs, but are punished for sexual misconduct and physical crime."

Reading this, I asked myself: Is this literally true? Is it even kind of true?

But then I read on:

"Similarly, on the world stage, Moslem extremists may not bomb New York, but rational human beings—some of them, to their shame, Jews—hold that they may bomb Jerusalem. These apologists are or pretend to be incapable of differentiating between the lamentable and decried death of civilians in a military reprisal, and the targeted murder of schoolchildren."

And so, the reader must ask himself, as I did: What do you think now?

"Here's the thing," Mamet said of the opening of "Well Poisoning." He explained that he was greatly influenced by such "American free-thinking philosophers" as Eric Hoffer, Emerson and Thorsten Veblen and by Veblen's style of writing in particular, which he described as "say[ing] things that blow your socks off, and you think about them and say, ' Oh my God, that's true.'" Mamet then quoted Hoffer, as saying, "People say the artist has the ability to see the future. That's not true. The artist has the ability to see the present."

"What I'm endeavoring to do [in *The Wicked Son*]," Mamet concluded, "is to tell the truth as I understand it in a responsible way and in a way which is responsible to my understanding of the needs of my people."

Mamet explained that his wife, actress and singer Rebecca Pidgeon, played an important part in strengthening his own connection to Judaism. About seventeen or eighteen years ago, when Pidgeon was taking an "introduction to Judaism" course,

Mamet realized that he had a lot to learn. Pidgeon is a Jew-by-choice, and Mamet said Jews-by-choice set a strong example because, "Jews-by-choice lack conflict" regarding being Jewish. Beyond that, Mamet noted, "my wife and I have been fortunate to study with two great and seminal thinkers in Reform Judaism, Rabbi Larry Kushner and Rabbi Mordecai Finley." ("The Wicked Son" is dedicated to Mordecai Finley and Finley's wife Meirav.)

Finley is the leader of Ohr HaTorah in Los Angeles, a congregation that describes itself, per its ohrhatorah.org Web site, as "a progressive, yet deeply religious community" having "a dedication to Jewish tradition, with an openness to modernity when it brings enhanced meaning and depth to our practice" and as welcoming "all who are spiritually searching; such as unaffiliated individuals or families and Jews-by-choice." Mamet has described Finley as a "spectacular teacher."

Although Mamet writes about Jewish ritual, about bar mitzvahs and synagogues, he wanted to make clear that the point of the book is not to criticize someone's practice (or lack thereof).

"If someone says I'm Jewish, but I'm not that Jewish. Who asked?" Mamet explained. "That's none of my business." He's not interested in what makes a Jew or how much of a Jew you are—that's between a person and his God. Mamet's point is different. Does anyone ask an Irish American, Mamet asks, how Irish they are? Or a Greek American or a Mexican American? They each love America and they cherish their heritage. Mamet asks: "To what other group do we say: Where do your loyalties lie?"

On the other hand: "If someone says ' I'm Jewish but I'm not that Jewish,' that is in the nature of a confession not a description." Mamet said. "It connotes a sense of shame." In other words, a manifestation of Jewish self-loathing.

"The point of my book is that the disaffected person may consider himself the victim of too much Judaism," Mamet said, "but someone who makes that confession has too little Judaism." Similarly in another passage, Mamet writes, "' Jewish Guilt' is not a side effect of being Jewish, but of being insufficiently Jewish. Buddhism will not cure it, self-help will not cure it, good works will not cure it, A Course in Miracles will not cure it—all of these, ranging from religion to nostrum, cannot eradicate the lapsed Jew's sense of being lost. For he is lost."

Mamet has been living in Los Angeles for several years now. Although at first he resisted the city, he now says, "It takes some getting used to. It's a different culture. I like it."

He commented on how he found the organic intellectual life of the city as "still growing, still defining itself," in a way that New York no longer was, and how Gore Vidal had called LA "the cultural capital of the world." "I've been thinking a lot about that," Mamet said. For the last several years, he has also been studying jujitsu. Mamet has written an article for the December Playboy about the sport and the Gracies—the Brazilian martial arts family who modernized the sport, went on to dominate Ultimate Fighting Championships and who has a substantial beach head in LA (I know this because I do read the *Playboy* articles—and because Mamet gave me a copy.)

In the article Mamet confesses to being pugnacious, and certainly *The Wicked Son* is testament to that. In jujitsu, then, I thought I had found a metaphor for Mamet's book and his relationship to Judaism. However, when I pointed this out to him, referring to Jacob who wrestled with an angel and was given the name Israel, Mamet's response was: "Interesting point, but no."

A few seconds later, he relented, saying: "In terms of physical grappling, no; in the sense of spiritual grappling, sure. To wonder about one's self and one's tribe and one's relation to God and the value of one's deeds is not something that keeps one from religion, but it is religion. That's what religion is; it is what the whole Torah is." Perhaps there's also a parallel to be found in Mamet's show, *The Unit,* about a group of men, a combat unit, who keep their identity hidden but are loyal to their country, to each other, and who act when called upon, when others are in danger, no matter where in the world. Is this the sort of tribal loyalty Mamet is searching for?

Then I realize why what Mamet is searching for ultimately doesn't matter, as he might be the first to tell you. What matters are the questions he is asking in his book.

We live in a time when anti-Semitism is no longer a matter of quotas or numerus clausus, of Nuremberg laws, or pogroms. We live in a country where one can say with conviction: It can't happen here. Where one can argue that there has never been a better time or a better country in which to be a Jew. But that doesn't mean that anti-Semitism is not occurring or that Jews are not being murdered) for the crime of being a Jew in Pakistan (Daniel Pearl), France (Ilan Halmi), or in Israel (I regret that the names are too many to list and that the casual anti-Semitism of certain academics, or in foreign newspapers is as any less pernicious or dangerous than what is being spewed in Iran or in radical mosques the world over. History has taught us that words lead to actions. In times like these, as Mamet might ask, should we be more Jewish or less Jewish?

At times like these, just as our love for our country, America, transcends the actions of any one administration—or any select individuals serving in Washington, Iraq, Guantanamo Bay or Abu Ghraib—should those who disagree with individual policies of the democratic government of Israel feel less solidarity with their fellow Jews or more?

I have heard the story of the four sons explained as a tale of the generations of Jews in a country—the first brings with them the customs and practices of the old country and the old religion; the next (the wicked son) rejects the old ways to make his own path in the new land; the next can no longer understand what the rituals meant; and the fourth generation is so cut off from its traditions that it doesn't even know how or what to ask about them. Is this our future or our present?

The challenge facing this generation, facing every generation since Egypt, is the same: To make of Judaism a living religion; to recognize that assimilation need not mean ignorance; and, in our generation, to foster a Zionism in a post-Zionist era, when moving to Israel is no longer the ultimate goal but standing in solidarity with Israel and its people remains central to our identity and our survival.

Whether you read David Mamet's book or not, whether you find it right on or over the top, whether you buy a copy for your friends to please them or infuriate them, the question, remains:

In or Out?

November 9, 2006

OLD JEWISH JOKES

Let us quote from sacred text: the 2005 Emmy Award acceptance speech by *Daily Show* host Jon Stewart. Spaketh Stewart:

"When I first said that I wanted us to put together a late-night comedy writing team that would only be eighty percent Ivy League-educated Jews, people thought I was crazy. They said you need ninety, ninety-five percent. But we proved 'em wrong."

Welcome to Jewish jokes in the twenty-first Century. Not really a joke, more of an observation really—and the funny part is that the joke is about being a majority not a minority. The Stewart quote appears in the recently published twenty-fifth anniversary edition of *The Big Book of Jewish Humor,* edited by William Novak and Moshe Waldoks (HarperCollins). If you want to laugh, or know someone in need of a laugh, you would do well to order a copy—or a dozen—as *The Big Book* is destined to become a popular gift item for friends and relatives.

The Big Book of Jewish Humor is a treasury of recent comic quotes, classic Jewish jokes, and selections from great comic writers from Sholom Aleichem to Israel Zangwill, from Woody Allen to Allen Sherman, from Groucho Marx, S.J. Perelman and George Kaufman to Saul Bellow, Philip Roth and Bernard Malamud, from Bruce Jay Freedman to Lenny Bruce, Leo Rosten and Sam Levenson. The margins are filled with commentary and more jokes from ancient to recent sources—calling to mind that tenth-century French wit Rashi's claim that "all else is commentary."

How can I squeeze into a few paragraphs all the jokes about Minsk, Pinsk and Chelm? All the tales that begin "Two Jews are on a train..." Perhaps I could just give the punchlines such as "You see, it's already starting to work"; or "My dog is dead! I was bringing her to Israel to bury." Or "Yossi put away your siddur, our prayers are answered"; or "Sadie, I'm beginning to think you're bringing me bad luck." My guess is that some you know, most you don't.

In their very funny introduction to the new edition Novak and Waldoks discuss what has changed in the twenty-five years since their book was originally published (beyond the fact that Waldoks is now a rabbi, and Novak became, as I like to call him, "the king of the ghostwriters," helping such diverse personalities as Tim Russert, Tip O'Neal, Lee Iacocca, Nancy Reagan, Rudy Giuliani and Magic Johnson become successful authors). One of the changes is that twenty-five years ago a few comics still told jokes.

"Remember jokes?" Novak and Waldoks ask. Blame it on George Carlin and Steve Martin, or Jerry Seinfeld and Steven Wright, but by the early 1980s comics had dispensed with the one-liners and stories that were the stock and trade of Borscht Belt, nightclub and television comics, and found a more conceptual, observational brand of humor that appealed to younger audiences. Comedy has never been the same.

But those jokes are missed, and not only by me. New Yorker writer Adam Gopnik, in his recently published collection *Through the Children's Gate* (Knopf), includes a chapter called "Purimspiel," in which he waxes nostalgic about the comedians who populated *The Ed Sullivan Show* with their "bits" and narrates how in the course of writing a performance piece for a Purim party, his relationship to Jewish jokes rekindled his dormant Judaism and Jewish affiliation.

For me, it is not so much the comics of the *Ed Sullivan* era that I hanker for, as it is the old Jewish jokes that inspired them. In matters of jokes, as in much else, I remain old school (I'm the sort of person who reacted to the passing of Jerry Garcia by commenting, "What I miss is Pig Pen").

Once upon a time, it seems to me, jokes were not the stuff of which to make a career from the Catskills or in Vegas or on television, but an oral tradition, an alternate education that occurred not just on holidays but at the dinner table or when a group of friends got together. Jokes were told and traded and found for all occasions and situations.

These jokes were spiked with wisdom. Some were self-mocking, others mocked the ruling order. At their best, they revealed a shimmer of truth and gave pleasure and comfort to teller and audience alike.

At one point last summer, in a wave of manic enthusiasm (and self-delusion), convinced that the fact that no one performed this material any more created a market opportunity, I took it upon myself to gather the greatest "Old Jewish Jokes"—thinking I might go so far as to actually revive the genre single-handedly by performing them myself.

My research uncovered a number of compilations, such as *Alan King's Great Jewish Jokes Book* (Crown) and *101 Classic*

Jewish Jokes by Robert Menchin (Mustang). I also found books that sought to explain Jewish jokes, such as Joseph Telushkin's *Jewish Humor: What the Best Jewish Jokes Say About the Jews* (Harper Perennial) and Arthur Asa Berger's *The Genius of the Jewish Joke* (Aronson). However, much to my disappointment, although there was quantity, many of the jokes were old saws that could apply to any ethnic group—they lacked that special quality to be found in the best old Jewish jokes.

The best collection I found was Henry Spalding's *Encyclopedia of Jewish Humor* (Jonathan David). It was there that I found the oldest Jewish joke to my taste. It is long, and were I to tell it in person it would be longer still. But to serve up its essence, the story concerns Eleazar, a Jew in Roman times, 100 B.C.E., who finds himself before the gates of heaven, ready to meet his maker, when he is stopped by the patriarch Abraham, who tells him that to meet the Lord he must be worthy of the honor and must recount an instance of bravery.

Eleazar relates that once he found himself before the Roman emperor, and to his face he told him he was a camel's behind, an oppressor of the Jews of Jerusalem and spat in his face.

Abraham is impressed: "When did that occur?" he asks.

Eleazar responds: "About ten seconds ago."

If that doesn't make you smile, then I can't help you. I would say that maybe you should see a psychiatrist, but in the course of my research I discovered that none other than Sigmund Freud was a great lover of Jewish jokes. Freud actually considered publishing a collection of his favorite Jewish jokes in the late 1880s, years before he published *The Interpretation of Dreams.*

Even after he achieved fame, he continued to consider the importance of Jewish jokes.

In 1905, the same year Freud published his book on the Dora case, and his landmark *Three Essays on the Theory of Sexuality,* he also published a volume titled, *Jokes and Their Relation to the Unconscious* (Norton).

Although a serious work, Freud did manage to work in some of his favorites, including jokes about schnorers (freeloaders), shadchens (matchmakers) and rival businessmen. One of the jokes that Freud rates as "excellent" is as follows, and I quote the good doctor:

"Two Jews meet in a railway carriage at a station in Galicia. 'Where are you going?' asks one. 'To Cracow' was the answer. 'What a liar you are!' broke out the other. 'If you say you are going to Cracow, you want me to believe you are going to Lemberg. But I know you are going to Cracow. So why are you lying to me?'"

Freud's interest in such jokes has itself been the subject of much interpretation. Elliott Orring in *The Jokes of Sigmund Freud* (University Press of Pennsylvania) makes a persuasive case that Freud's own concerns about Jewish identity are intertwined in his interest in old Jewish jokes.

Which brings me back to why jokes disappeared. I was once derided in a national publication for daring to tell a George Jessel joke by a self-anointed "connoisseur of comedy." (Apparently the barb still stings.) With 20/20 hindsight, I can see that, for a time, the comics of the *Ed Sullivan* era, the Henny Youngmans and George Jessels had become too embarrassing—too "ghetto" (in the original Italian sense).

It is also possible to argue that old Jewish jokes were the language of outsiders, a coping mechanism for a culture of potential victims. Michael Vex, in his excellent *Born to Kvetch*

(Harper Perennial) makes the case for an attitude, a spirit that might no longer exist in a world where our children are happy all the time (i.e., they love school, they love after-school, they even love religious school).

Why would anyone growing up today suspect that someone who says they are going to Cracow is lying to them? (They would say: "Where's Cracow?")

At the same time, as Novak and Waldoks point out, while the comics became less directly Jewish in their material and how they told it, the popularity of such shows as *Seinfeld, Curb Your Enthusiasm* and *Everybody Loves Raymond* are an indicator of just how suffused with Jewish humor American society has become.

Phil Rosenthal, the co-creator of *Everybody Loves Raymond,* in his charming and comic memoir, *You're Lucky You're Funny* (Viking), makes clear how having parents who survived the Holocaust is a sitcom (as if that wasn't obvious). For Rosenthal, humor comes from the specific.

If you need further proof of what I like to call "the Bagelization of America," let me give a literal example and remind you of a popular series of TV ads that appeared every few minutes on TVs all over the country (and still does)—for Jimmy Dean pork sausages on a bagel. Need I say more?

However, what goes around comes around. *The Big Book of Jewish Humor* has better jokes than any work I consulted, including Freud. However, as Novak and Waldoks make clear, if they were assembling a *Big Book of Jewish Humor* of the twenty-first century, they would include fewer texts from novels and more material from the Internet.

Today, old and new Jewish jokes are making their way around the World Wide Web, becoming once again evergreen.

As anyone who finds themselves in front of a computer screen knows, retro or contemporary, old school or new, there is something of value in a joke—if only the ability to laugh.

Perhaps Novak and Waldoks' twenty-fifth anniversary edition of *The Big Book of Jewish Humor* is the start of a Jewish joke revival. I hope so. Maybe one day I'll actually take the stage and utter those words made famous throughout history: "I'm available also for bar mitzvahs, weddings and social occasions. Order the veal."

December 7, 2006

SWIMMING IN THE HOLOCAUST

Recently, I attended a screening of *Swimming in Auschwitz,* a still unreleased documentary directed by Jon Kean about the experience in the Auschwitz-Birkenau camp of six women—Eva Beckmann, Rena Drexler, Renee Firestone, Erika Jacobi, Lili Majzner and Linda Sherman—all of whom survived and today live in the Los Angeles area.

The film is notable for sharing the woman's experience of the notorious camp.

Kean succeeds at having the women speak with candor about their families and their experiences as the war took hold, and how the Nazis put them in ghettos, on the transports to Auschwitz, as well as about their arrival and their tribulations there.

Kean records their histories with great respect and compassion for the individual spirit of each of the women involved.

The documentary's title comes from an anecdote Jacobi relates about one hot August day when, as she was marched from her barracks, she was taken past the German officers' swimming pool. Although taking any step outside the ranks could have meant death, impulsively, she dove in the pool, swam to the other side, got out and rejoined the march. The guard said nothing.

The anecdote is not meant to serve up any greater truth. It represents just one unusual occurrence. Yet, as a metaphor, to be "swimming in Auschwitz" is an apt description of the experience of watching the documentary.

There is nothing easy about watching a documentary about Auschwitz, not even a well-made one. Already knowing the facts about the camp and what the inmates endured takes nothing away from the shock of hearing the specifics of their experience.

As I watched the film, I was overwhelmed by the realization that the time for such documentaries was almost up; that within a decade or two there will be no more eyewitnesses to the crimes. But I was also thinking about the Holocaust itself, and how my feelings about the events described have changed over time.

That night I went home and fell asleep, only to wake in the middle of the night. I stumbled out to our living room, stretched out on the couch and reached for a book that I had been avoiding for several months, the new edition of Elie Wiesel's *Night* (newly translated from Wiesel's original manuscript by his wife, Marion).

I had read the book in high school but remembered little of it. Now, I read the book in one sitting. *Night* is Wiesel's account of his incarceration in Auschwitz and Buchenwald. Wiesel was a teenager at the time, a devout, religious boy, and his account seethes with anger at God and at himself, as he witnesses the death of his family members and as he becomes a person who survived Auschwitz.

In the preface to the new translation was a simple sentence by Wiesel: "Only those who experienced Auschwitz know what it was. Others will never know."

There it was: the truth about the Holocaust. What I realized, and this is something that I have been struggling toward for a long time, is that the more I know about the Holocaust, the more I read, the more documentaries or movies I see, the more I have come to grasp that the Holocaust not only defies understanding; it demands that we admit to and respect the fact that we can never truly understand what occurred.

My parents both lived through the Holocaust (neither in camps), and I grew up surrounded by survivors and their families. I've spent many, many hours listening to survivor accounts. I was active in children of survivor groups and attended several survivor gatherings.

I wrote a book about a Nazi war crimes trial, for which I interviewed several survivors of the Treblinka extermination camp and read the testimonies of many more. There is a sea of Holocaust material in which I have been swimming for much of my life.

As a subject hovering near my consciousness, I have at times attempted to push it away and other times drawn it close. But although it has never been far away, my own thinking has evolved over the years.

My father was a resistance hero, so as a child, I thought of the Holocaust as a James Bond story, where my father vanquished the evil Nazis through his cunning and his smarts; a Purim story in which Hitler was Haman, and the Jews triumphed over their enemies. In my late twenties, I thought of the Holocaust as a call to bear witness and to engage in social action. In my thirties, I came to think of the Holocaust as a diabolical criminal enterprise in which the murder and attempted extermination of the Jewish race was preceded by plundering their wealth and possessions.

All of which is a long way of saying that despite what I've read, seen, heard or learned, or perhaps because of it, I find myself less and less willing to find a moral or a lesson or some meaning to the Holocaust. Perhaps, that's out of increased wisdom or deeper insight. Most likely, it's just my getting older.

But I ask myself: How could so psychologically complex and nefarious a plan been carried out involving so great a mass conspiracy and such mass cooperation, support and acquiescence? How exactly could the architects of the , so called, final solution conceive of and then involve so many in acts that no one believed could possibly occur, while relying on the optimism and disbelief of their intended Jewish victims to lead those unfortunates into the snare of death?

How can one comprehend the levels of inhumanity man could visit against man? How can one imagine the perverse creation of factories of death with their multiplicity of stratagems for humiliation and dehumanization, for turning man against man, and inmate against inmate, for the varieties of death in a system that culminated in murdering Jews and then insisting on killing them again by cremating their bodies (an added affront to Jewish tradition and law)?

How can you understand being there, dying there or even surviving being there? Did the Nazis really believe that they could in this fashion erase all evidence of the murders and of their victim's existence? Even if their purpose was murder, the rituals and routines of Auschwitz made no sense whatsoever. Yet the mountain of facts are alarmingly rational. We, who were not there, can never really enter the nightmare world. Yet the facts of the Holocaust, once known, can never really leave our consciousness.

I have come to resist exactly what I was guilty of, of making the Holocaust into a teaching story. The late Susan Sontag, in her essay, "Against Interpretation," argued that the methodology of art theory is based on a premise that requires art to justify itself. Using her logic, it behooves us to ask ourselves why we expect the Holocaust to have a justification? I believe it is because we, who can never really understand it, feel compelled to create theories about why it occurred for the sake of our own humanity.

What I wish is that we could separate the Holocaust from our response to it. We have the facts. They are enough. We don't need to spin them—to posit the Jews who were murdered as sheep who were led to slaughter or as martyrs or heroes. We need only pay respect to the facts themselves, free from interpretation.

But I know that it is impossible. The very incomprehensible nature of the events and the legacy of the murder impel us to seek ownership and control of the horror by coloring the events with our response to it. That is as understandable as it is inevitable.

Wiesel writes in his new introduction that "having survived, I needed to give some meaning to my survival." Wiesel became a writer and then an advocate, an outspoken moral voice speaking out against anti-Semitism and the crime of potential genocide wherever it occurred—for which he received the 1986 Nobel Peace Prize.

The women in *Swimming in Auschwitz* became mothers and grandmothers. That, too, is a response. They lived when so many imagined they would not. They have shared their tales as a legacy for the generations to come.

For the survivors, telling their stories, recording their histories and memorializing the dead have given lie to the Nazis' boasts that no one would remember and no one would care. Out of respect for the survivors and for the dead, we, too, are impelled to document, to remind, to remember.

For those born after the Holocaust, those who will only know of the Holocaust from the testimonies of others, from books, and teachers and documentaries and movies and miniseries, I can only hope that when they dive into the pool of Auschwitz information, they will come out the other end and continue to march on, respectful of what they can never understand, not so much changed as needing to respond.

December 21, 2006

LITERARY PAPRIKA

What better way to start the New Year than by sprinkling a little literary paprika?

Consider this: Mark Sarvas, a New York-born son of Hungarian parents, a voracious reader, a Francophile and a foodie, comes to Los Angeles to be a writer, sells some screenplays and starts an acclaimed literary blog, The Elegant Variation (marksarvas.blogs.com/elegvar).

To top it all off, Sarvas has just completed his first novel, as yet untitled and currently being submitted to publishers. *Yoy Ishtenem*! If ever there was a ready-made subject for Tommywood, this is it.

Let's begin with some background.

Sarvas' father was born in Budapest, his mother in Vienna, and both grew up in Budapest. On his mother's side, much of her maternal family was murdered at Auschwitz, and her father spent much of the war in forced labor, arriving eventually at Mauthausen, where he was liberated at war's end. Sarvas' father's family lived under false papers in the country during the war, and it was Sarvas' father's task to smuggle food for them.

His parents married in 1955 and divorced a year later. Sarvas' father left Hungary the next year, following the 1956 revolution. Sarvas' mother came to the United States in the 1960s. They reunited in New York and remarried. Mark Sarvas was born soon thereafter. As he told me, that tale, in of itself, could make for a novel.

Sarvas' own story is rich with foreshadowing of his literary interests. He was born in Manhattan at a hospital on East 30th Street that no longer exists, The French Hospital. His mother tells an apocryphal story that as a one-year-old, he ate the frontispiece page of *The Complete Works of Shakespeare,* predestining him for life as a littérateur.

Sarvas, however, credits a high school creative writing teacher with steering him to writing (and away from the rock band that was consuming his energies). That, and reading F. Scott Fitzgerald's *The Great Gatsby* as a sophomore at New York University, which "set a fire" within Sarvas to become a writer. (As noted in his blog, Sarvas re-reads *Gatsby* every January to begin the New Year—more on that later). He began writing short stories and went on to become managing editor of the NYU paper, The Washington Square News.

Upon graduating in the fall of 1986, Sarvas came to Los Angeles with the promise of co-writing a script for the TV show, *Moonlighting.* Although, as they say in California, that didn't pan out, Sarvas did begin to write scripts.

Aided and abetted by his agent (now manager) Steve White, he joined the league of screenwriters who make a living, but whose work rarely gets made or read by more than a cadre of industry folk. He was writing, but was he expressing himself?

Someone famously said that Los Angeles is a pool where you dive in at one end and come out the other to find twenty years have gone by. As the twenty-first century dawned, Sarvas found that he had become a fan of literary blogs, online personal diaries that refer to, quote from and comment on writers—the blogger reviews and writes while often narrating his or her own travails and adventures in the writing world. Sarvas admired Maud Newton's www.maudnewton.com/blog and Laila Lalami's Moorish Girl blog, www.lailalalami.com/blog/.

One day—October 14, 2003, to be precise—feeling that he had something to add to the literary conversation, Sarvas launched The Elegant Variation blog. The rest, as they say in the blogosphere, are entries.

"I had no idea what I was getting into," Sarvas now says.

The Elegant Variation, according to Fowler's and as cited on Sarvas' blog, refers to prose that calls attention to itself. Sarvas' interest is in fiction that does the opposite, so I can only assume that he is being self-deprecating about his talents, ambitions and the inherent potential pretension of being a literary blogger. Sarvas' blog appears over pleasing shades of green background.

The center features his daily digest of news (i.e., Salman Rushdie's next work will be a historical novel), comments about reviews, literary prize winners, obits, new books, events, all featuring links to the those texts. On the left side of the Web page are books Sarvas is currently recommending, such as a new collection of Paris Review interviews, *The Mystery Guest* by Gregoire Bouillier and *Ticknor* by Sheila Heti.

As blog entry followed blog entry, Sarvas realized that he had a unique perspective: "I could provide coverage of L.A authors and LA events," he said.

For a while, he ran a Monday morning critique of the Sunday *LA Times* Book Review, but he stopped to give the section's new editor, David Ulin, time to find his footing. Now that more than a year has passed, Sarvas is considering starting up again.

He also tries to highlight authors and items of literary interest that are, "further afield." He championed the British author John Banville long before the Booker Award committee anointed him.

Sarvas' blog is in the process of running an in-depth interview with Banville and in the past has featured interviews with authors such as Andrew Sean Greer (*The Confessions of Max Tivoli*). A recent interview with Jonathan Lethem broke the news that Lethem is introducing a Philip K. Dick anthology.

Sarvas feels that "he's at the right place and at the right time," he said. He believes "there's an evolving sense of a literary community," both in Los Angeles and in cyberspace. In that regard, he was also instrumental in founding the Litblog Coop (lbc.typepad.com), a blog that recommends contemporary fiction.

Part of what Sarvas most enjoys about his blog is the friends he has made and the correspondences he has had with readers from all over the world. He has even engendered a literary dust-up with another blogger—not quite Mailer vs. Vidal or a Trump vs. Rosie fracas but still evidence of the growing pains of an ever-expanding community.

The Elegant Variation has no commercial dimension—no ads or banners. Sarvas makes "not a dime," from the blog, he says. It is "a labor of love." For this writer, at a time when literary books no longer hold the general culture in thrall and in a city where many sit alone in rooms wondering, in the words of E.M. Forster, "how to connect," it is reassuring to read a blog where someone cares about literature and those novels that may never make the best-seller lists.

Beyond that, I feel a certain kinship with Sarvas, based on our shared backgrounds. Reading his blog makes me want to call out, much as Baudelaire addressed his reader, "Hypocrite lecteur, mon semblable, mon fr?re"—not only because I want to amortize my expensive education, but also because I am confident that Sarvas would get the reference.

It is easy for me to imagine the two of us in Budapest 100 years ago, scribbling our feuilletons in the corner of a café, rather than in Los Angeles, each in our own corners of the increasingly wide world Web. If any of the Hungarian Jews who came to Hollywood in the 1930s and 1940s were young men today, wouldn't they be writing literary blogs? In this way, I look at the whole notion of creating The Elegant Variation as an essentially Hungarian enterprise.

At the same time, it is also very LA This is the City of Dreams in the State of Self-Invention (Just consider our governor, for starts). It is also a place where one person can still stand out and stake a claim. In that sense, The Elegant Variation is very much of California and of LA

But to really understand why people still come to Hollywood, and why they continue to pitch and write on spec, or still write literary novels and/or start blogs—and continue to do so in the face of the changing industry—you have but to turn to Sarvas's favorite novel, *Gatsby* (and let's not forget that Fitzgerald himself ended his days here). Is there a better explanation for the essential optimism that animates our lives and that inspires Sarvas and "The Elegant Variation" than how Fitzgerald concludes his great novel?

"Gatsby believed in the green light, the orgiastic future that year by year recedes before us. It eluded us then, but that's no matter—tomorrow we will run faster, stretch out our arms farther.... And one fine morning—"So we beat on, boats against the current, borne back ceaselessly into the past."

January 25, 2007

I WAS A TEENAGE PUNK

Recently I asked a fifteen-year-old boy what music he listened to. His answer: "No one you ever heard of." A perfect answer. Because what every fan needs, what every person should have, is music that is his own.

Over the years, there's been a lot of music that has mattered to me. That I have enjoyed; that I have loved. But if you asked me what music was mine—I would name without hesitation a bunch of bands that first flourished in New York in the late 1970s, such as The Talking Heads, Television, Richard Hell and the Voidoids, Blondie and the Patti Smith Group.

I don't listen to them much these days, but that doesn't matter. There was a moment in time when I was so deeply connected to what they were doing, their music and their ambition, that it seemed they were playing the soundtrack to my life.

Secretly, I believed that I had discovered these bands; whereas in truth, I had probably first read about them in the Village Voice or the Soho News (as if I were the only one reading those publications). I heard Patti Smith reading poetry at the St. Mark's Poetry Project and purchased a copy of *Witt*, a collection of her poetry that featured a Polaroid cover portrait by would-be photographer Robert Mapplethorpe, at the Gotham Book Mart. I was at one of Blondies' first performances Upstairs at Max's Kansas City (The Runaways opened for them). Each weekend and many a weeknight was a search for the music of my times, as I stood by the wall or on my seat in clubs and concert halls, such as Hurrah's, The Mudd Club, Danceteria and the Academy of Music (which became the Palladium).

It might have been the place, or the time, or the time of my life, but the bands were smart, ironic, disaffected and spoke to my privileged New York bourgeois conflicts and alienation. They sprang from The Who, but their references included Verlaine and Rimbaud. They were different; they were unique; they were creating a tribe of their own.

Or at least I thought so. However, according to a new book I am reading, "The Heebie Jeebies at CBGB'S: A Secret History of Jewish Punk," by Steven Lee Beeber (Chicago Review Press), it turns out that what I shared with many of my musical idols was that we already were members of a tribe.

Beeber, whose work has appeared in *The New York Times* and The Paris Review, makes a compelling case that New York punk owed a lot to the Jewish backgrounds (hidden or acknowledged) of Lou Reed, Lenny Kaye (Patti Smith Group), Chris Stein (Blondie), Jerry Harrison (Modern Lovers, Talking Heads), Joey Ramone, Tommy Ramone, Sylvain Sylvain (New York Dolls), Johnny Thunders (New York Dolls), Jonathan Richman (Modern Lovers), Alan Vega (Suicide), Handsome Dick Manitoba (The Dictators), Malcolm McLaren (Sex Pistols impresario) and Hilly Kristal, owner of CBGB's.

As Beeber tells it, New York punk was born of the Lower East Side, the shtetl of the golden land, and forged by the children of Jewish immigrants as a post-Holocaust response to the

Jewish American dream of assimilation and success.

Charting a course from Lenny Bruce to Malcolm McLaren and filled with profiles of the major bands of the era (Suicide, The Dictators, The Ramones, Blondie) and interviews with many of the original participants and their cohorts, Beeber's book occasionally reads like a theory in search of the facts to support it. A point he addresses in the book, asking and deflecting a possible charge that he is merely reducing these artists to a link many of them would not acknowledge as meaningful.

But that doesn't stop Beeber, who goes on to argue that even denying one's Jewish background is a Jewish thing to do—which reminds me of George Steiner's famous quote that the twentieth century showed that being Jewish was not a club one could resign from. Nonetheless, the more one considers Beeber's argument, the more persuasive it becomes, not only as an explanation of Jewishness or punk but of human nature.

We would all like to believe that we are unique—yet, at the same time, we are part of a mass culture. We each dress in our own way, putting on clothes that more often than not are produced for a large group of consumers. The music we like, the movies and shows we watch, even the foods we love, those things that define our taste are more often than not all created for an audience greater than ourselves.

At the same time, in an increasingly fragmented society, we find comfort in brands, in belonging to tribes. The pierced and the tattooed recognize each other, as do the Prada and Marni clad. We need to be different even as we need to belong.

I once spent an afternoon interviewing Ralph Lauren, philosopher of style semiotics, who explained to me that fashion is all about one question: When you close your eyes, what sort of person do you see yourself as? Uptown or downtown? Businessman or gangster? Similarly with music you might ask, are you a Beatle or a Rolling Stone? A White Stripe or a Raconteur? Or as a soft drink ad once put it: "Are you a Pepper?"

We may listen to a lot of music, but when we close our eyes, which band or artist is our secret self?

Turns out the musicians and singers who made the music that I consider mine, and that I, in my secret self, still belong to were each, in their own way, nice and not-so-nice Jewish boys rebelling against their backgrounds and their times. They were searching for the transcendent and the transgressive, and channeling their talent and, at times, their self-loathing into a way to be different than who they were supposed to be.

Punk was an act of rebellion. Still, as Beeber reveals, their music struck a chord reaching back into their personal histories and created for me, as much as for them, a way to belong.

February 1, 2007

ASSUME EVERYONE IS JEWISH

A couple of weeks ago I found myself in a seminar room at UCLA's Royce Hall attending a presentation by professor David Shneer of the University of Denver concerning Jewish museums in Los Angeles, a city he calls, "The Newest Jewish City in the World."

As someone who has argued that Los Angeles is the premier Jewish city of thetwenty-first century, I was eager to find academic support for my own theories.

Everyone thinks of New York as the most Jewish city (outside of Israel), and that may be true in terms of population and certain ethnic benchmarks, such as the quality of bagels, number of delis and access to good Chinese food.

However, historically, Jews in New York have been a vibrant minority who, for most of the twentieth century, remained outsiders—only recently reaching the upper echelons of business, politics and society. Growing up in New York, the people I knew were Jewish, but I believed everyone else was not Jewish—until proven otherwise.

Similarly, it seemed that in order to rise in New York, you had to pass for WASP. Why else would anyone care about Ralph Lifschitz taking the name of Ralph Lauren (and/or snicker about it)? Why, even in this day and age, would Vanity Fair get mileage out of Tory Burch being Jewish?

Los Angeles is the opposite. Although it has its own history of prejudice and restricted clubs, Jews have been part of Los Angeles since its founding (there was a Jewish member of the first city council in 1850). Perhaps it is because Jewish immigrants founded the movie business, but in Los Angeles, I assume everyone is Jewish.

Los Angeles is also the greatest Hispanic city in the United States ... and the greatest African American city...and the greatest Asian city—that is part of what makes Los Angeles great, that each person can call the story of Los Angeles his own. However, my experience in Los Angeles is that if you take the most non-Jewish person you know, regardless of race, religion or ethnic origin, inevitably you will run into them at a bar mitzvah only to discover that their spouse, stepparent, grandparent, grandchild or nephew is Jewish, or that they are converting. It's uncanny. Perhaps it is no accident that the Kabbalah Centre chose Los Angeles as its headquarters and launching pad. Madonna as Esther, Demi wearing her red string, Britney wearing her Jewish star—it's very Los Angeles, no?

But let's return to the more academic approach.

LA native Shneer, whose presentation was based on his book *New Jews* co-authored with Caryn Aviv (New York University Press), made the case that historically, mass emigrations of Jews have occurred due to politics or persecution—consider the Babylonian exile, the expulsion from Spain following the Inquisition, as well as the wave of immigration at the end of 19th century that brought Russian and Eastern European Jews to the United States and South America. This also applies to the flight of Soviet Jews between 1989 and 1991.

By contrast, less studied but equally notable, Shneer argued, were the post-World War II patterns of migration that have led so many Jews to choose to live in Los Angeles. "LA is deeply studied among American historians, but little studied among Jewish historians." Shneer said.

Shneer noted that in 1900 the five largest Jewish population centers were New York (500,000), Warsaw (220,000), Chicago (220,000), Budapest (200,000) and Vienna (200,000). In 2000, the top five were: Tel Aviv (2.5 Million), New York (1.9 million), Haifa (655,000), Los Angeles (621,000), and Jerusalem (570,000). Hence the title "Newest Jewish City in the World."

Statistics from the City of Los Angeles reveal that Jewish population jumped from 65,000 in 1930 to 315,000 in 1950 to 565,000 in 2000, at times accounting for 18 percent of the population. (This just refers to the City of Los Angeles, and doesn't include those independently incorporated cities with substantial Jewish populations such as Beverly Hills, West Hollywood or Santa Monica, as well as the Valley communities.) For the purpose of the survey, "Jewish" was self-identified—so if you said you were Jewish, they took you at your word.

Perhaps we should call Los Angeles "The Chosen City."

Shneer's thesis is that once upon a time synagogues revealed Jews' communal identity, but today for most American Jews, it is through their Jewish museums that they present their identities to the world and themselves. Shneer believes this is particularly true in Los Angeles, as evidenced by the Museum of Tolerance and the Skirball Cultural Center, each of which reveals different attitudes about being Jewish and about the relationship of Jews to the outside world.

The Simon Wiesenthal Center's Museum of Tolerance—Beit Hashoah (its full name)—was founded by Orthodox Jews, is closed on Saturdays, is located near the Pico-Robertson neighborhood and houses a yeshiva on its grounds. Given its pedigree and its focus, as found on its Web site, to "confront the dynamic of intolerance that is still embedded in society today," you might think that the content of the museum and its attendees would be overwhelmingly Jewish. Yet the museum exhibitions appear geared to non-Jews, focusing on tolerance and civil rights, and most days bring in a constant stream of inner-city school visits. Shneer argues that the museum's message of tolerance can be interpreted as a manifestation of a contemporary Orthodox attitude: i.e., because we are different, we need to live in a tolerant society.

By contrast, there's the Skirball, which was founded by Reform Jews and is located near Mulholland Drive and the 405, between the assimilated Jewish enclaves of Brentwood and Encino. Open on Saturdays, the center promotes itself as a place to celebrate the connection between Jewish heritage and American democracy. Shneer argues that the Skirball presents a Reform point of view: "of acculturation without assimilation." The message is that we are all Americans, yet—in contrast to the Museum of Tolerance—its visitors and the focus of its exhibits are overwhelmingly Jewish.

"Despite its marketing efforts to position itself as a place for everyone," Shneer has written, "the museum is obviously Jewish."

Both of these institutions, in their own way, are temples to Jewish life in Los Angeles.

In the great tradition of two Jews, three opinions, it should come as no surprise that Shneer's seminar had its share of dissenters. David N. Myers, director of UCLA's Center for Jewish

Studies, for one, suggested that Shneer's distinctions were simplistic and that the two institutions could just as easily be seen as presenting two differing narratives of the Jewish experience, one lachrymose (the Museum of Tolerance), the other triumphalist (The Skirball).

At the same time, Tal Gozani, the Skirball's associate curator, noted that the Skirball has evolved since Shneer's research concluded in 2003. She also pointed out that the Skirball's permanent and temporary art exhibitions are but one facet of an institution that offers music, dance, film and spoken-word performances. In July, the Skirball will open an ambitious "Noah's Ark" family gallery, Gozani said, which will engage children in many subjects, including zoology and the environment, but which, save its name, will offer up no specific Jewish religious references from the Torah.

Shneer responded that both Myers and Gozani's comments on the respective institutions were, in fact, completely in keeping with their origins—a view of Jewish history as a litany of persecutions is congruent with an Orthodox interpretation, while treating Noah's Ark as a "flood narrative with counterparts in many cultures" sounded like a Reform approach.

For my part, I saw in Shneer's comments a greater truth and a greater challenge than even he acknowledged.

Los Angeles is not only a city where Jews present their identity through Jewish museums; it is also a place where Jews have had an unparalleled role in shaping the cultural identity of the city. Jews here have been instrumental in establishing the majority of the city's art museums, including a significant number serving as trustees and professional leaders at the Los Angeles County Museum of Art, the Norton Simon Museum, the

Museum of Contemporary Art (MOCA) and UCLA's Hammer Museum. Jews have also played a role at The Getty Trust under the stewardship of Harold Williams and Barry Munitz. Add to that Eli Broad's role in the construction of Walt Disney Concert Hall, and as a founding trustee at MOCA, as well as the donor of $50 million to build the Broad Contemporary Art Museum, still under construction at LACMA, and a remarkable portrait of the "Newest Jewish City" emerges.

Still, I was struck by Shneer's remark that "synagogues used to be the places in which Jews constituted their communal Jewish identities."

He's right, of course. It used to be that if you were a big shot, you gave to the synagogue.

"If I were a rich man," sang Tevye, I would "have a seat by the eastern wall." Which led me to think: Why does each Jewish billionaire need his own museum? When being Jewish is part of the culture, what if culture (and the cultured) returned the favor?

Why can't Jewish synagogues also be showcases for culture?

Imagine, for a moment if you will, if Broad, who is reportedly going to help underwrite a multi-multimillion dollar Jeff Koons sculpture of a life-size functioning steam train engine that would hang from a crane in front of the entrance to LACMA, were to give $50 million to the renovation and restoration of the Wilshire Boulevard Temple (which I have been told has the second-best acoustics in Los Angeles, after Disney Hall).

How many temples could be restored, how many liturgical, musical and cultural programs could be funded by David Geffen, Mike Ovitz, Marcia Weisman and the host of other big museum donors and creators.

Audrey Wilder just gave $5 million to create the Billy Wilder Theater at the Hammer Museum; what if, instead, that theater was just down the road at Sinai Temple? More recently, Sheldon Adelson, of the Las Vegas-based Sands corporation, pledged $25 million a year for the next several years to support the Birthright program sending youths to Israel, and, in December, rumors were flying that he was planning to give as much as $200 million annually to support Israel and foster Jewish culture. He denied the rumors, and no such announcement has been made—but, as is often the case in Hollywood, I believe the rumors will, in time, prove true. If they do, will any of these dollars go to support Jewish culture at American synagogues? (And equally important will any of it go to supporting Tommywood? Not completely on point—but I couldn't resist.)

In Los Angeles, "the Newest Jewish City," Jews are shaping the culture, and their Jewish museums are shaping our notions of Judaism in American culture. Can Jewish culture also play a role in revitalizing our temples?

To quote Lerner and Loewe (whom you may assume were Jewish): "Wouldn't it be loverly?"

March 1, 2007

ALSO BY TOM TEICHOLZ

*Greetings from Tommywood (*Volume One). Pondwood Press, 2015.
Tommywood III: The Column Strikes Back! (Volume Three). Pondwood Press, 2015.
Tommywood Jr., Jr: The Gospel According To Tommywood (Volume Four). Pondwood Press, 2015.
Fast Furious Tommywood (Volume Five). Pondwood Press, 2015.
Close Encounters of the Tommywood Kind (Volume Six). Pondwood Press, 2015.
Wilshire Boulevard Temple and the Warner Murals: Celebrating 150 Years by Tom Teicholz, Oro Editions, San Francisco, CA 2014.
The Jewish Role in American Life, Casden Insitute Annual Study, Volume 1, by Barry Glassner, Hillary Lachner, and Tom Teicholz, USC / Casden Institute, Los Angeles, CA, 2008.
Like No Other Store: Bloomingdale's and the Revolution in American Marketing by Marvin Traub and Tom Teicholz, Times Books/Random House, New York, New York, 1993.
The Trial of Ivan The Terrible: State of Israel vs. John Demjanjuk by Tom Teicholz, St.Martin's Press, New York, New York, 1990.
Conversations with Jerzy Kosinski, edited and with an introduction by Tom Teicholz, University Press of Mississippi, Jackson, Mississippi, 1993.

Conversations with S. J. Perelman, edited and with an introduction by Tom Teicholz, University Press of Mississippi, Jackson, Mississippi, 1995.

Other books and anthologies containing Tom Teicholz's work:

Encyclopedia Judaica, Second Edition. Tom Teicholz, American Film and TV editor., 2006.

Conversations with Isaac Bashevis Singer, University Press of Mississippi, Jackson, Mississippi, 1992.

Writers at Work, Volume 8, The Paris Review Interviews, Viking/Penguin, New York, 1988.

ACKNOWLEDGEMENTS

I want to thank the Rob Eshman and Susan Freudenheim at *Jewish Journal of Los Angeles* for providing Tommywood with a home and Roy Sekoff and Kimberly Brooks at *The Huffington Post* for letting me reach an even larger audience; the publicists and communications executives who aided me; the friends who suggested stories and the stories which became the basis for new friendships; and my wife Amy and daughter Natasha for being good sports about it all.

I also want to thank the contributors to The TOMMYWOOD Collection IndieGogo campaign for their support and generosity which made publication possible, most notably my tzadiks, hoochems and benefactors: Sandy Climan, Bracken Darrell, Lawrence Schoen, Toni and John Schulman, Bob & Cori Davenport, Peter Graham and Heidi Drymer, Ken & Teri Hertz, Wally & Helen Weiss, Dede Arnholz, Chuck Leavitt, Sharon Nazarian, Chris Pilkington, Stacy and Massimo Pinello, Robert & Edie Parker, Annie Scichili, and Richard Wolloch.

There is more to a book than just writing its content. You need talented people to successfully prepare it for publication. The reason this book looks so terrific is because of designer Devin Tanchum and the very talented folks at Rare Bird Lit, notably my book guru Tyson Cornell and his excellent associates Alice Elmer and Violet Sarosi, as well as Winona Leon (who did the design work for my IndieGogo Campaign). I also want to thank John Vaskis and John Trigonis at IndieGogo for teaching me so much about crowdfunding and helping make this book possible.

ABOUT THE AUTHOR

Tom Teicholz is an award-winning journalist, producer, and content consultant who has created print, video, and social media content for Intel, Logitech, The Museum of Tolerance, and The Milken Family Foundation as well as for several not-for-profits and private clients. His work has appeared in *The New York Times* Sunday magazine, *The Los Angeles Review of Books*, *The Los Angeles Times* Op-Ed page, Newsweek.com, *The Paris Review, The New Yorker's 'Talk of the Town', Narrative Magazine*, Forbes.com and the *Huffington Post.* He lives with his wife and daughter in Santa Monica, CA.

www.ingramcontent.com/pod-product-compliance
Lightning Source LLC
Chambersburg PA
CBHW021507110726
47899CB00001BA/326

* 9 7 8 0 9 8 8 3 9 6 4 6 3 *